PAULINE BRYAN, Baroness Bryan of Partick, i
campaigner. She was nominated for a life pe
Leader of the Labour Party in May 2018, ma
the abolition of the House of Lords. She is part of the Red Paper Collective
and has written extensively on constitutional reform.

Pauline Bryan is a founding member of the Keir Hardie Society, and was
the editor of the 2015 book *What Would Keir Hardie Say?* and in 2019
Keir Hardie & the 21st Century Socialist Revival. She has a chapter on
Keir Hardie's first election campaign in 1888 in the forthcoming book *By-Elections: The 87 By-Elections That Shook British Politics* edited by Iain
Dale.

Keep Left

Red Paper on Scotland 2025

Edited by

PAULINE BRYAN

Luath Press Limited

EDINBURGH

www.luath.co.uk

First published 2025

ISBN 978-1-80425-206-2

FSC
www.fsc.org
FSC® C023367

The mark of
responsible forestry

Printed and bound by
Robertson Printers, Forfar

Typeset in 11.5 point Sabon by
Main Point Books, Edinburgh

Contents

Acknowledgements

THANKS TO DENISE Christie, Stephen Low, Coll McCail, Vince Mills and Frieda Park for bringing together the authors in their sections. I received a huge amount of help from Peter Duffy who proofread the whole work several times and suggested many improvements. Thanks to everyone at Luath Press for their help in particular Amy Turnbull, Kira Dowie and Jennie Renton.

Foreword

AS GENERAL SECRETARY of the Scottish Trades Union Congress, I'm acutely aware of the importance of *The Red Paper on Scotland* to my organisation and the wider labour and trade union movement. The original *Red Paper* played a crucial role in shaping the thinking put forward by my predecessors for a Scottish Parliament – one that could protect the real wealth of the Scottish people – workers and their families.

While we helped achieve a Scottish Parliament, we are still some distance from a worker's parliament. That is why this book is so timely.

Of course, a lot has changed since 1975. This was a time when the 'irresistible march' of nationalism and industrial unrest, wrote Gordon Brown, could be moulded in a socialist direction. But while it struck a positive tone, the *Red Paper* wasn't naïve. It forewarned of the issues facing Scotland: ever greater external control of our economy, oil subverting Scotland's manufacturing industry, and the rise of nationalism uprooting the British political order. All these trends have not only accelerated but remain relevant today.

That pessimism of the intellect, optimism of the will which seeps through the original *Red Paper* is needed now more than ever. Because 50 years on, the most likely 'irresistible march' seems to be that of the far right.

People are fed up with the British state. But they are increasingly fed up with the Scottish state too. The centre-left politicians of these islands are in the last chance saloon. If they let our people down, then our people will look to the far right for answers, and this danger is growing greater every day.

That is why the visionary proposals put forward in this Red Paper are so important. Because it is only through real substantive change that addresses the material concerns of ordinary people that we will stop the far right from gaining ground.

And there is no shortage of visionary proposals in this book. In pulling it together, the editor, Pauline Bryan, has done a great service to the labour and trade union movement.

Thankfully, the contributors are more diverse than the original *Red Paper*, but they all share the desire for radical redistribution that the original reflected.

Pauline Bryan, Salvador Allen Hughes, James Mitchell, Katrina Faccenda and Matt Kerr pick up the themes of democracy articulated 50 years ago by Gordon Brown and Tom Nairn and consider the need for change at UK, Scottish and Local Government level.

Stephen Low, Susan Galloway and Dave Watson consider how we rebuild our public services, hollowed out by 40 years of underfunding and outsourcing.

Vince Mills, Costas Lapavitsas, Richard Leonard and Sara Cowan revisit, in a modern context, the theme of social control over our economy, including in social care and manufacturing.

Frieda Park, Diarmaid Kelliher, Lynn Henderson, Thomas Morrison and Arthur West pick up the gauntlet from trade union titans such as Alex Ferry and consider how we can reinvigorate our trade unions and exert workers' control over industry.

Coll McCail, Andrea Bradley, Rosie Hampton and Gavin Brewis trace out where we are and where we should go in relation to our education system, energy transition and the criminalisation of young people.

Denise Christie, Susan Morrison, David Archibald, Núria Araüna Baró, Tommy Breslin and Julie McNeill consider the unique power of culture to challenge, unite and transform – whether that be in the theatre, on our screens, through music or in our football stands.

And I can think of no one better than John Foster, a contributor to the original *Red Paper*, to close the book.

Not everyone will agree with everything written, but I have no doubt that these are the real debates and discussions that we need to have if we are to reverse the irresistible march of the far right, and deliver a fundamental shift in income, wealth and power towards workers, our families, and communities in Scotland and beyond.

As we stand on the cusp of further industrial and political change, I hope this *Red Paper* will have as significant an impact on the trade union and labour movement, and wider Scotland, as the original.

Roz Foyer
General Secretary, STUC
March 2025

Introduction

THIS BOOK IS AN invitation to everyone who is concerned about politics today to join the discussion about where we go from here. We need to remember the times of optimism as well as gloom. Central to any rejuvenation is revitalising democracy which means being involved not just when casting an occasional vote but seeing the opportunities and challenges in our communities, workplaces and the wider world.

Celebrating a book that was published 50 years ago, while trying to make it relevant to readers born this side of the 21st century is a challenge. The writers in this book believe that many of the issues that impact on life today were set in motion at the very time when Gordon Brown was bringing the authors together to produce the *Red Paper on Scotland* in 1975. So, while we mark its 50th anniversary, we try to understand its relevance for today and for the future.

The British and Scottish left at the time of the book's publication seemed supremely confident that the world was theirs to win. The young Gordon Brown, as Student Rector of Edinburgh University, was a perfect expression of that confidence. He succeeded in bringing together 28 academics, trade unionists, and other writers (all of them men) to contribute to this seminal book. It followed on the heels of the successful Upper Clyde Shipbuilders work-in. The excitement that success generated was infectious. Not only had the 'work-in' tactic spread but its leaders, particularly Jimmy Reid, became TV personalities.

The share of national income paid to workers peaked in the mid-'70s and has been in decline since. The powerful trade union movement of the 1970s sustained not only high wages, but high social benefits in healthcare, education and social welfare. The Labour Party, returned in two elections during 1974, was compelled by trade union campaigning to repeal the Tories' Industrial Relations Act that had tried to restrict the right to strike.

Optimism was bolstered by any number of socialist journals and newspapers as well as left bookshops giving space for lively debate. At this time of heightened political interest, *The Red Paper on Scotland* was an important publication; it helped create, not just catch, the mood of the day.

Few of the commentators at that time imagined that four years later Labour would lose power to the widely reviled Margaret Thatcher 'milk snatcher' and that it would be a further 18 years before Labour would once again win power. And could they have imagined the changes there would be during those years to society, to politics and to Gordon brown himself – from radical rector to conservative chancellor?

Despite the victory for the Tory government in 1979, Labour won the popular vote in Scotland. For the next three UK general elections Conservatives won across the UK while Scotland continued to vote Labour. The Tories went on to impose unpopular policies on Scotland; the Poll Tax, privatisation of utilities (except for water which was successfully resisted) and gerrymander local government with the abolition of Regional Councils.

The divergence between voting in England and voting in Scotland made the demand for devolution unstoppable, but the Scottish Parliament was shaped at the time of New Labour and was not the radical 'workers' parliament' envisaged in the 1970s.

Ironically, the Parties that gained the most from the new Parliament were two parties that had initially opposed it – the Conservatives and the SNP. The Conservative Party returned 18 members to the first Scottish Parliament in 1999 despite their obliteration in the 1997 Westminster election and ultimately went on to replace Labour as the official opposition to the SNP in 2021. The SNP used the Scottish Parliament as a platform to build support for independence, largely by winning working class votes for what it presented as a social democratic alternative when New Labour was adopting neo-liberal ideas.

The Labour Party was taken unawares by the successful leadership campaign of Jeremy Corbyn in 2015. That short period brought many people into political activism for the first time and could have built a movement for change. For some people the undermining of the campaign left them disillusioned, but others were determined to learn the lessons of that time to prepare for future opportunities. They lost, but they learned.

The 2024 UK general election saw a big drop in the fortunes of the SNP: it was reduced to just 9 Westminster MPs, down from 48 in 2021. This, and the general turmoil within the Party, may suggest that it is a party in decline, and that Scottish Labour will be well placed to win the largest number of MSPs in the Scottish Parliament in 2026. As it stands, however, Scottish Labour under Anas Sarwar will have to offer a much stronger vision for the future to overcome the disappointment voters feel with the UK Labour Party.

The international situation is bleak. Progress on climate change has stalled and the right is gaining power across Europe encouraged by Trump's nation first politics. All this, and the lack of progressive polices in the UK or in Scotland, creates what some call a 'doom loop'

So here we are at the 50th anniversary of the *Red Paper on Scotland*, but now at a time when there are few illusions that either the SNP or Scottish Labour have plans for radical change. It is clear from the polls that the electorate has lost faith in both parties, and we may even see the Reform Party winning seats in Scotland.

This book presents a different vision for Labour, a vision full of hope, enshrined in the ideas of the founders of the Scottish and British Labour movement. The authors of this book believe only a radical redistribution of wealth and power within a democratic economy and society can realise that vision, and only a campaign for an economy dedicated to people's needs will engage Scottish voters.

As we write, Scottish Labour is preparing a manifesto for the 2026 Scottish Parliament elections. It must decide whether it has a programme for the people of Scotland that dares to be different from the Westminster government.

Against this backdrop, this version of the *Red Paper* looks ahead to what positive options are available for the future.

As Gordon Brown wrote in 1975:

The social and economic problems confronting Scotland arise not from national suppression nor from London mismanagement (although we have had our share of both) but from the uneven and uncontrolled development of capitalism and the failure of successive governments to challenge and transform it.

Where now for Scotland?

There is a clear theme running through the book, and that is democracy. The use of the word has become narrow and applied to formal, political, electoral arrangements but the chapters in this book broaden it to mean empowering people to be active participants rather than passive recipients. It must also refer to economic control and to redistribution of wealth. Unequal societies cannot deliver full democratic participation. From local government to industrial development, from education to environmental campaigns, these issues are too important to be left to a technocratic elite. Democracy should include subsidiarity, enabling power to be exercised at the level closest to the people it affects.

Approaching the elections for the Scottish Parliament in 2026 the parties will be judged on the visions they have for giving power to people. A new government must recognise the urgency of transforming politics so that it isn't captured by the right.

A future Scottish government must:

1. Use the powers it already has to tackle economic decline and failures in services. It should introduce a wealth tax and fairer taxation policy as outlined by the STUC in *Raising Taxes to Deliver for Scotland.*
2. Demand borrowing powers for rebuilding public services and infrastructure.
3. Introduce a gender-equal economy that benefits everyone, particularly paid and unpaid carers and those experiencing economic inequality.
4. Develop an industrial strategy with a focus on democratic, strategic economic planning. This should include a role for trade unions and community movements.
5. Have the authority to enhance trade union rights beyond UK levels, but never below.
6. Revitalise local government. Unelected boards, whether at the Scottish or local level, must be held accountable to elected representatives.
7. Give local government powers to take the lead in municipal ownership of services and utilities.
8. Provide long term investment in arts and culture making art available to everyone.
9. Demand the right to participate in international trade negotiations and decisions on international policies to ensure that Scotland's needs and values are represented. It should also have the authority to issue visas for migrants to live and work in Scotland.
10. Work with the other devolved administrations to demand the abolition of the House of Lords and its replacement with a Senate of the Nations and Regions. This must be safeguarded by a codified UK constitution that prevents power grabs from the tier above.

Pauline Bryan
March 2025

Timeline

1971–72 Upper Clyde Shipbuilders Work-in is a victory for trade union organisation.

1974 Labour Party narrowly wins 2 General Elections. SNP win 11 seats in October.

1975 Referendum on membership of European Community. Workers' controlled newspaper launched.

1975 *The Red Paper on Scotland*, edited by Gordon Brown is published. It's called 'a landmark publication'.

1976 Labour Government takes IMF loan in exchange for large cuts in public spending.

1979 Referendum on a Scottish Assembly. A narrow win for 'yes', but the requirement that 40% of whole electorate is needed to win, means it is overturned.

1979 SNP support vote of no confidence in Labour Government which results in a general election.

1979 Margaret Thatcher wins general election. Introducing privatisation of utilities, the right to buy council houses and attacks on trade unions.

1980 Launch of the Campaign for a Scottish Assembly. It adopts the 'Claim of Right for Scotland'.

1984–1985 Miners' strike. The defeat results in widespread social and economic devastation.

1989 The Scottish Constitutional Convention outlines a voting system for a future Scottish Assembly.

1997 Labour wins the general election with commitment to referendums for Scotland and Wales. Tony Blair is Prime Minister and Gordon Brown Chancellor of the Exchequer.

1997 Two question referendum in Scotland: 'Should there be a Scottish Parliament?' 74.9% say yes. 'Should it have tax raising powers?' 63.5% say yes.

1999 First Scottish Parliamentary election. Labour wins 56 seats and forms coalition with LibDems. Donald Dewar is First Minister.

2007 Tony Blair resigns as Prime Minister Gordon Brown replaces him.

2007 Scottish National Party wins most seats in Scottish Parliament. Governs as a minority party. Alex Salmond becomes First Minister.

2007–2009 Worldwide economic crisis caused by banks but impacts on vulnerable economies and working people worldwide.

2010 Tories win general election. David Cameron and Chancellor George Osborn impose austerity.

2011 SNP win overall majority in Scottish Parliamentary election. Alex Salmond claims a mandate for referendum on independence.

2014 Referendum on Scottish Independence. 'Should Scotland be an independent country?' 44.7% in favour 55.3% against. Alex Salmond stands down replaced by Nicola Sturgeon.

2015 General Election disaster for Scottish Labour as it only holds one seat. SNP have 56 MPs.

2015 Jeremy Corbyn elected leader of the Labour Party. 2017 Richard Leonard elected leader of the Scottish Labour Party.

2020–2021 Keir Starmer elected leader of UK Labour Party. Anas Sarwar elected leader of Scottish Labour Party.

2023–2024 Nicola Sturgeon resigns as First Minister, Humza Yousaf is elected. Power sharing with the Greens breaks down. Yousaf resigns and is replaced by John Swinney. Police investigate SNP finances.

2024 General Election. Labour wins a big majority. Scottish Labour returns 37 MPs, SNP 9.

Gaining Powers, Losing Control

Introduction

Pauline Bryan

IN 1975 IT seemed inevitable that a Scottish Assembly would be established by the Labour Government before the end of its term. Gordon Brown and many of the other authors in *The Red Paper on Scotland* wrote with a belief that they were on the cusp of a new relationship between Scotland and the UK Government.

It turned out to be a critical time, but not for the reasons they had anticipated. Labour's defeat in the 1979 election was not reflected in voting in Scotland, where Labour gained seats. The Thatcher Government seemed determined to change the political culture of Scottish politics through local government reorganisation, industry closures, privatisation and austerity. What it achieved instead was an increase in support for devolution.

The question running through many of the chapters in the original *Red Paper on Scotland* is how the voices of working people can be heard. The three chapters in this section, under the heading 'Gaining Powers, Losing Control', explore the same issue.

It has been an interesting five decades for Scottish politics. Just four years after *The Red Paper on Scotland* was published there was a referendum on devolution that was effectively scuppered by George Cunningham, a Labour MP, born in Scotland, but who represented an English constituency. He, like a number of Labour MPs, was opposed to devolution, and he successfully introduced an amendment to the legislation on the 1979 consultative referendum on Scottish devolution to nullify the result if support for devolution was less than 40 per cent of the total electorate. This not only prevented the establishment of a Scottish Assembly, but eventually brought down the Labour Government.

The 1997 referendum creating a Scottish Parliament has been described as a constitutional response to a political problem. There was such hostility in Scotland to the Thatcher and Major governments that nationalism was winning support, not just among Labour Party supporters, but among Labour Party members. Support for independence in that period peaked at 47 per cent in Ipsos polling in 1998 but fell quickly soon after, though not to the extent predicted by Labour Minister George Robertson that devolution would 'kill nationalism stone dead'.

Looking back at the debates in the Westminster Parliament it was clear that there was a lack of clarity about the nature of sovereignty in the UK, and no recognition that such a significant change in the constitution implied a move towards a federal UK and shared sovereignty, with implications for England and the make-up of the second chamber.

Once the honeymoon period of having Labour in power in both Westminster and Holyrood (as well running most of the larger Scottish local authorities) was over, the tensions between the three layers of government began to test the fragile constitutional structure that had been established.

The three chapters here cover the three layers of government in Scotland and their impact on people's lives.

Starting with local government, which is where most political engagement takes place, Katrina Faccenda and Matt Kerr, as local councillors, experience the daily frustrations of responsibility without power. They make the point that councils have been stripped of powers and subjected to greater scrutiny than any other level of government. Powers have been diverted to other bodies such as Integrated Joint Boards and City Region Deals that take decisions without being accountable.

The Scottish Government's priorities are often imposed on local government with ring-fenced funding attached, limiting further already stretched budgets. Faccenda and Kerr argue that there is a real possibility that councils will be reduced to an extension of the Scottish Government without a political voice or role to represent local interests.

The Scottish Parliament was shaped by discussions held a decade before its introduction in the Scottish Constitutional Convention. As James Mitchell describes in his chapter, the Convention wanted to avoid some of the faults in the Westminster Parliament which had such low representation of women and ethnic minorities. The Convention was however later described by John McAllion MSP as elitist. That may have been unfair, but as James Mitchell points out, little thought was given to class. This could have been because it wasn't thought necessary as it was expected to be, in the words of STUC General Secretary Jimmy Jack in 1972, a 'workers' parliament'.

It is understandable that a devolved parliament sandwiched between the UK government and local government would feel the need to stretch its reach both upwards and downwards. It has demanded and to some extent received greater powers, while having others clawed back by central government. For its part, as described earlier, it conducted its own power grab on local government.

James Mitchell argues for the reassertion of a commitment to subsidiarity that was part of the raison d'être of devolution. Subsidiarity in theory should devolve powers to the lowest level where they can be used effectively, but this commitment has been lost. He also argues that the power within the Scottish Parliament has become unbalanced. The founders pictured a strong effective legislature able to hold the executive to account through its committee structure. Instead, the Scottish Government has been able to rely on the 'payroll vote' and a weak committee system, to be largely untroubled by accountability.

The consequences of not holding a government to account, regardless of its political colours, are seen in the poor outcomes in the economy and public services.

The level with the greatest power and most distant from the electorate is the UK Government. Salvador Allen Hughes has written on how the lack of a codified constitution has contributed to the UK being one of the most centralised governments in an advanced democracy. That remains the case even after devolution.

Hughes makes a strong case for economic democracy being as necessary as political democracy. The unaccountability of central government has allowed it to become obedient to the interests of finance capital to the detriment of the UK economy as a whole.

He argues that political change should be more pluralistic and locally accountable, suggesting three routes to greater participation. Firstly, proportional representation; secondly, introducing participatory budgeting in local government; and thirdly, by primaries for the selection of candidates for election.

The two local councillors raise concerns about how people are represented in local decisions and make a case for activism, rather than passive representation through citizens assemblies. There is also a case for the right of party members to choose their candidates but, as Hughes argues, this must require party members to have genuine control of the process.

Whether it is the constitution of the state or of political parties Gordon Brown was right when he wrote in his introduction to *The Red Paper on Scotland*:

The question is not how men and women can be fitted to the needs of the system – but how the system can be fitted to the needs of men and women.

Fighting for Local Democracy

Katrina Faccenda & Matt Kerr

LOOKING AT THE current state of local government in Scotland it is difficult not to ask where it all went wrong. From the struggle to deliver the most basic services, the visible decay of the fabric of our cities and the difficulty in identifying one council in Scotland that has a clear strategy to implement something anywhere close to the municipal socialism of the '80s, there is little evidence of progress and much evidence of decline.

For decades councils have been stripped of powers and subjected to greater scrutiny than any other level of government. Today's large, multi-councillor wards have diminished the role of a councillor as a local champion. Political parties are indifferent, failing to develop strategies for local democracy and confirming the lack of value they give it. How has this come about?

The Wheatley Report in 1969 recognised that something was seriously wrong with local government in Scotland and suggested that the root of the problem was principally structural, highlighting an imbalance of power with UK central government. It also noted the low public standing of councillors with the consequential difficulty of attracting good quality candidates. The subsequent *Local Government (Scotland) Act* of 1973 eventually led, two years later, to the two-tier system of nine large regional and 53 district councils. One benefit of large regional authorities was their ability to redistribute resources from well-off to poorer areas.

During the Thatcher years, the political debate on the left in Scotland focused on devolution versus independence, pushing aside issues around improving the structure of local government. The Conservatives under John Major needed little encouragement to abolish regional councils, as the majority were controlled by Labour and a fair few of the Labour councillors were still fighting for jobs and services. Like many attempts to reorganise local government, it was carried out when central governments saw it as a threat to its interests.

The current arrangement in Scotland was imposed in 1994 by the Major Government, intending to extinguish once and for all the spirit of resistance in local government which had survived Thatcher's rate-capping, poll tax, imposition of competitive-tendering, and decimation of block grants. Poorly evidenced accusations of high bureaucratic costs and wasted money were used as a front for dismantling the two-tier system and, with it, the ability to redistribute. Since some of the new authorities were too small to take on all local authority functions some powers were transferred to the Secretary of State, to joint boards and other forms of joint delivery. It was the beginning of a significant shift of power away from elected members to bureaucracy and quangos. Integrated Joint Boards and City Region Deals mean decisions on spending and strategy are taken without full democratic accountability.

Any hope that the establishment of the Scottish Parliament would result in further devolution and redistribution of power to local government has been buried. There has been no major legislation from the Scottish Parliament to restructure local government, and the endless and often costly discussions and consultations around community empowerment remain meaningless without reform of the mechanisms that could implement them. The erosion of local authorities' powers has been accompanied by additional responsibilities to deliver the priorities of central government, with a growing chunk of funding ring-fenced to do this, meaning that councils have become delivery bodies, rather than a form of government.

When the Scottish Government has considered subsidiarity and local government, the latter is often presented as incapable, incompetent and profligate. MSPs and MPs assume that it is their right to hold councillors to account rather than that of local electors. The Best Value duties introduced under the *Local Government in Scotland Act 2003* demand that local authorities develop arrangements to demonstrate continuous improvement in their performance but leave them with an endless and expensive series of audits. It could be argued that it takes some nerve for the Scottish Government to place duties of 'vision and leadership' and 'effective use of resources' on local government while it is failing in these same duties.

The *Community Empowerment (Scotland) Act 2015* was described as helping to empower community bodies through the ownership of land and buildings, and by strengthening their voices in the decisions that matter to them. Instead, it has become just another method to bypass and undermine councillors. Although presented as progressive, community empowerment is often used to strip powers from councillors and transfer them to individuals and self-selected groups of people. Asset transfers may give communities possession of their own buildings but are more likely to push unwanted responsibilities onto communities forced to deal with a threat of closure, or to pass valuable assets to the private sector.

The 2020 revised statutory guidelines for Best Value were presented as guidance to help local authorities and other public bodies demonstrate continuous improvement in their performance. They may have been described as a gold standard approach to financial responsibility, but the demand for alignment between a local authority's budgets and its strategic priorities has allowed bureaucrats to block the political aspirations of democratically elected representatives. Councillors should feel angry at how Scottish governments have continuously dictated to local government.

Meanwhile, councils remain under-funded and unpopular as they implement the cuts passed down from central government, increase the charges for their non-statutory services and raise council house rents to balance their budgets. The Confederation of Local Authorities (COSLA) does in theory represent councils, but it seldom operates as an instrument of collective strength to demand more powers or to reform the broken funding system. When Holyrood politicians make decisions to freeze the council tax, they deny councils vital funds and blatantly disrespect the rights of democratically elected councils.

One of the first issues facing the new Scottish Parliament was its relationship with Scottish local government. The 1999 McIntosh Commission on Local Government identified the loss of local discretion over revenue raising, introduced under the Tories, as having undermined the credentials of local government – but the call for a review of local government finance was not accepted by the then Labour led Scottish Executive, and had to be taken up by the Local Government Committee of the Scottish Parliament.

In 2002 the Committee's Report made the case for other forms of taxation in addition to council tax including land tax, local income tax, sales tax and a service tax as well as a council tax revaluation. Instead, the *Local Government in Scotland Act 2003* gave powers to raise fees and income, often leading to those least able to afford it being charged higher fees for access to non-statutory services like libraries and sports. Report after report has agreed that councils should have more power to raise revenue and that it is for their electorate to hold them to account on how council budgets are spent and how funding is raised. Twenty-two years later all we have is the option of a transient visitor levy which is welcomed by councils like Edinburgh but will not touch the sides of councils' deficits.

Instead of exploring ways of bringing power closer to our communities, the discussion in the Scottish Labour Party has become sidetracked on to whether we need metro mayors. This idea may appeal to those who want to emulate the celebrity status achieved by some successful metro mayors in England. It does, however, fail to consider several factors, including: the role of the Scottish Parliament; whether cross-council City Region deals have achieved anything significant; why we need another, less accountable, layer of government – particularly one where politics is reduced to a beauty parade and personality stifles debate on policy.

A similar debate occurred in 1999 at the time of the McIntosh Commission on Local Government when in the early days of the Scottish Parliament the idea of directly elected council leaders was considered. The concept seems to pop up every time the future of local government or indeed the future of democracy is discussed. It is the answer to everything and the solution to nothing.

The executive system is endemic in Scotland's local authorities and normalises the centralisation of power providing the perfect 'gateway drug' to encourage the move to elected mayors. There is a new caste of politician who has experienced 'the taste of honey' – having power without those awkward committees that stop them getting things done. It is a small step from this to supporting the role of metro mayors.

Given that we have experienced years of decline in local government, have been fed on a diet of tales of council powerlessness, profligacy and bureaucracy and been alienated from the political process, it is hardly surprising that the idea of elected mayors proves such an easy sell. What it represents however, alongside the ever-growing quangocracy, is the triumph of the unaccountable executive over scrutiny, and status over substance; it's the final crowning achievement, the de-politicisation of everyday life.

The dangers of this should be obvious enough. No matter how much people may gaze longingly at the metro mayors of England, attracted by the seemingly unstoppable ability to deliver on policies like public transport, a pause for thought is required.

The entire edifice rests on the *West Wing* watcher's belief in the earnestness of it all; that those in a position to wield such power are not only the great, but the good, and that any tendency to excess can be dealt with, not by the wise counsel of an elected council, but by the expert 'staffer'. The answer to calls for action will come in poetry so photogenically delivered that any rank of question just melts away. It narrows the gene-pool of ideas to those who can win access to the chief, and any access that fellow elected members can achieve – whether on a council or parliament – soon competes with access gained through patronage.

Patronage conferred by the mayor to 'staffers', and patronage conferred on the mayor by business – it's so much easier when there's only one head to turn.

Debate matters, local input matters, workers' voices matter, and it is not just the mayoral system but also the executive system that undermines each of these vital democratic components.

Committees can be dull, tedious, and frustrating, all the more so for the growing lack of ability to chair them amongst the political classes. This problem is exacerbated by the belief that they are less a forum for debate and more a platform for social media clips.

It is worth considering the origins of elected mayors in recent political developments. The demand for elected mayors did not emerge from any great popular movement for better local democracy. There were no campaigns of any note to create them. The *Local Government Act 2000* began the job of undermining councils, forcing a move from committees to executives and from that position, it gave the option of a local referendum on a having a directly elected mayor. Since the establishment of the original metro mayors, the majority of referendums on creating elected mayors have resulted in 'no' votes. As of May 2024, 13 local authorities, all in England, have elected mayors.

Blair is often hailed as the Prime Minister who delivered devolution to Scotland and Wales, but in truth he was simply in post when decades of grassroots campaigning rendered those cases unanswerable. It is notable that, lacking the years of diligent campaigning and pressing of the case, similar later efforts to deliver regional assemblies in England fell flat on their faces.

We would argue that the revitalisation of local democracy must be central to the project of winning a socialist future; after all it is where the seeds of much of the social progress seen in the last century were sown. From housing and education to health and social work, the proving grounds have always been local. As have many of the battlegrounds.

But before the fighting begins, we need to know what we are fighting for. Community councils and tenants and residents' associations, imperfect as they are, were long the backbone of local democratic involvement. Councillors throughout the land were challenged face to face on their action or inaction at these meetings and kept informed of local issues that may not always have made it into the council inbox.

In recent decades that has begun to dwindle, creating a gap that in many communities has either gone unfilled altogether or been squatted on by so-called citizens' assemblies. These bodies are barely worthy of the name as hard-pressed communities are set against each other to compete for council grants or discuss precisely how they would like their services decimated.

Notable exceptions include Unite's community branches, tenants' unions and Living Rent, whose ability to organise door to door, close to close and street to street, mirror the methods and results of their antecedents who won social housing, rent controls and the vote in the early part of the last century.

Those experiencing the power of collective action in such organisations, often for the first time, must be at the heart of any socialist and democratic shift. The role of councillors in this instance must be as encourager, giving backing to whatever way people in their locality choose to organise.

Back at the chambers, executive, unaccountable, power must be dismantled wherever possible. If poseurs wish to use committees for social media, at least let us make sure that they are challenged and that the challenges matter. This will meet with resistance, not only from officers who have grown used to centring policy on pleasing a single cabinet member, but from some elected members who have either grown used to challenge being retrospective or would feel ill-equipped to make their case – itself a tragedy.

The democratising of outside boards must be central. Health and social care partnerships would not be a bad place to start. Glasgow's 85 elected members, for example, have no practical way to develop or scrutinise social care policy in the city, nor decide on a budget amounting to almost a third of its entire expenditure.

City Region deals are as opaque, undemocratic, and equally as susceptible to lobbying as the elected mayoral system. Their existence is a testament to how desperate councils have become after being dangled on the end of a string by central government through decades of power-grabs and cuts. The most important change that could come to councils in Scotland though, is for powers of general competence to return – powers enjoyed by almost all local authorities in the developed world.

Only now, after a decade of budgets being slashed, has the Scottish Government begun to consider devolving powers to councils on things like tourist taxes and congestion charging. While a reformed grants structure from the centre must remain as a vital corrective to deprivation and Scotland's very own uneven development, councils must be given the power to levy taxes appropriate to their locale at the level they choose.

This single step would open the possibilities for tax options on the likes of wealth either unavailable or unused by the Scottish Parliament, but above all it would give the voters real choices. Whether they organise to fight a local levy or to campaign for one, local government would move from being an arms-length cuts machine, to a centre of power that matters in every community. It could return local governments to where they once were, battlegrounds of ideas, centres of resistance where governments could meet their match.

That is of course why central government stripped so much from them, but if we are to reverse that, if we are to win any of the asks here, or turn the tide on decades of cuts, we need more than a shrug of the shoulders and a pained expression of powerlessness on budget day.

If we want to see and support communities coming to the fore, to see the needs, wants, and collective aspirations of the working class fulfilled, councillors must lead by example and use their mandate to fight for it.

After all, if councillors won't fight for local democracy, how can we expect anyone else to?

Holyrood and Westminster – Learning to Live Together

James Mitchell

THERE WAS ONE reason above all others for the emphatic endorsement of devolution in the 1997 referendum. Margaret Thatcher's period in power convinced many Scots that they needed some means of preventing the imposition of Tory policies, such as the poll tax, in future. The old Scottish Office had been established over a century before to acknowledge Scottish distinctiveness at the heart of government but this pre-democratic institution looked increasingly anachronistic, especially when the governing party at Westminster lacked support in Scotland. Eighteen years of Tory rule helped mobilise support for a Scottish Parliament that would be responsible for Scottish Office functions. The Scottish Parliament added a democratic element to a pre-existing arrangement. The demand for a Scottish Parliament was, however, defensive. There was less thought given to the kind of Scotland that a new devolved polity might help create.

The *Scotland Act 1978*, the original model of devolution developed in response to a surge in nationalist support in the 1970s, was dusted down and amended but there was less effort than needed to consider the purpose of devolution. Bolder ideas that had been considered in the early 1980s, including fiscal powers with devolution, seen as an 'important component of the Alternative Economic Strategy' by members of the Labour Coordinating Committee, were quietly dropped. But the incipient radicalism was later diluted. Emphasis was placed on symbolic change most notably in references to a Scottish Parliament rather than Assembly.

From 1989, the Scottish Constitutional Convention had deliberated on the form devolution should take. Its main contribution was in terms of representation. The emphasis was on party political, gender and ethnic minorities' representation. The Convention concluded in favour of the Additional Member System and greater representation of women and other groups that had been under-represented in the Commons. There was little thought as to class representation, reflecting the decline of class thinking generally. Debate on devolution's powers was limited. The working assumption was that Scottish Office responsibilities would transfer to the Scottish Parliament. Labour support for tax-*raising* powers in the early 1980s evolved into support for tax-*varying* powers in an effort to convey fiscal responsibility and reject Tory accusations that Labour was a 'tax-and-spend' party. The paltry tax-varying powers were more significant symbolically than useful policy tools.

Devolution was largely untested in its early years because Labour was in office in London and Edinburgh and, more importantly, this period coincided with significant growth in public spending. High levels of spending lubricated relations between London and Edinburgh. The financing through a base-and-formula mechanism, commonly known as the Barnett formula, meant that Scotland continued to benefit from historically higher levels of public spending than other parts of the UK. These conditions helped embed devolution.

But relations between Holyrood and Westminster deteriorated in more challenging times when the SNP gained office in Edinburgh and the Tories moved rightwards in London. Blame games replaced constructive joint efforts to address social and economic challenges. This was exacerbated when Brexit was used by the Conservative Government in London as an opportunity to reverse devolution, raising questions as to how to protect existing devolved competences.

There were modest policy initiatives and occasional conflicts with London. An obsession with policy divergence between Scotland and the rest of the UK (rUK) was probably inevitable amongst the commentariat but proved a distraction. In some cases, the divergence resulted from policy changes in London rather than Edinburgh. The introduction of tuition fees south of the border was not adopted in Scotland. The Scottish Parliament endorsed recommendations of a Royal Commission on Long Term Care for the Elderly, established by the Blair Government on coming to office, that were rejected by Westminster. Inevitably, there were conflicts. The issue was whether and how they would be resolved. Differences over the handling of the foot-and-mouth crisis in 2001, funding of policing at the g8 summit at Gleneagles in 2005, on regulation of airguns created some friction but never escalated into the kind of battles that would occur later. Policy aims were often shared and differences focused on how they should be achieved. That basic prerequisite of collaboration could not remove policy disputes but provided the basis for workable and constructive relations.

The real test of devolution came when the two conditions that had created a positive environment for good relations ended. In 2007, the SNP won one more seat than Labour in Holyrood with 47 of the 129 MSPs and formed a minority government. Three years later the Tories were returned in coalition with the Liberal Democrats at Westminster. Even more challenging was the economic and fiscal context. The sub-prime banking crisis that started in the US reverberated across the globe in 2007–9. The Royal Bank of Scotland, then claiming to be the world's largest bank and which politicians of all parties competed to be associate with, had to be rescued by the state along with other banks and building societies. The UK Government response was austerity.

Neither the SNP nor Tories wanted to be seen to undermine devolution initially. Each party had stood outside the Constitutional Convention and were perceived by many Scots who supported devolution as likely to undermine the devolved settlement for different reasons. The SNP was thought likely to pick fights with London at every turn in pursuit of independence. And the Tories, it was assumed, had not come to terms with devolution. Each needed to demonstrate that they would make devolution work if they had any prospect of building support. David Cameron's 'respect agenda' had its mirror in Alex Salmond's emphasis on governing devolution competently. The SNP was so successful in creating an image of competence that it won an overall majority in Holyrood four years after first forming a government. The 2011 election result, however, set Scotland on a different path. Respect was abandoned by the Tories and the SNP shifted focus onto the constitution.

The SNP manifesto commitment to an independence referendum played little part in the campaign and the constitutional question had declined in significance between the 2007 and 2011 elections but ironically the referendum was now firmly on the agenda. Buoyed up by polls showing support for independence at only around 30 per cent, Cameron agreed that a referendum would be held insisting that voters should be given a binary choice. Research shows that around a quarter of voters then supported independence when offered three options: independence, more powers or the status quo. The *status quo* and 'more powers' each had the support of around 40 per cent. The question was how the significant body of people who preferred more powers would behave.

In the event they split fairly evenly in the 2014 independence referendum though slightly more towards independence. The substance of 'more powers' was inadequately defined, reflected dissatisfaction with the alternatives and likely only found expression as 'more powers' due to the framing of the question and lack of an alternative means of expressing dissatisfaction. The constitutional framing of politics encouraged, if not forced, a choice at either end of a constitutional continuum.

There were different ways of considering devolved powers. From a nationalist perspective, it involved an insatiable accumulation of more powers with independence as the end point. But an alternative perspective saw government as a complex structure with a range of policy tools available, and decisions to be made on the most appropriate location of such tools. A third perspective added to the second and took account of political preferences, how powers would be used depending on location. Many Scots assumed that an empowered Scottish Parliament would be both able and willing to use its powers to create a fairer Scotland. This was based on an assumption that Scotland was more 'progressive' than the rest of the UK. The experience of quarter of a century of devolution has challenged that last perspective to some extent.

Before any list of further devolved responsibilities is drawn up it is important to consider the principles that should inform such decisions. A reassertion of the commitment to subsidiarity and how this can be embedded is essential. While subsidiarity is an essentially contested term – what one person sees as subsidiarity might be the opposite of others – this can only be resolved through evidence and argument. Subsidiarity has been invoked to claim more powers for European institutions by supporters of European integration, for returning powers from the EU to the UK by Margaret Thatcher, for devolution within the UK and for more decentralisation to local government. Subsidiarity only becomes meaningful with clarity of the purpose of government. Hence other principles must be taken into account. As an example, social and territorial justice is vital. It would be wrong to have a system that gives a wealthier area a major advantage by virtue of its wealth. This means that there will always be a central government role in providing equalisation to address fiscal disparities across the state. In essence a perspective is needed that is firmly embedded in the question of which competences or tools of government – taxation, spending powers, law-making, regulations etc – are required to deliver improved outcomes for citizens. This perspective must replace the constitutional lens through which debate has been conducted on devolved powers. Others may argue for additional principles to be considered and what is now needed is debate on such principles before demands for more powers.

Changes under the Scotland Act 2016 have left the Scottish Parliament with less money to spend on public services. The combination of SNP desire to accrue more responsibilities and the Treasury's willingness to concede responsibilities that would devolve difficult choices, has resulted in the Scottish Parliament gaining more responsibilities without compensatory powers. The challenges involved have been accentuated by a timid Scottish

Government that places more emphasis on performative politics than achieving improved outcomes. The emphasis on tax responsibilities rather than borrowing powers in debates on further devolution exemplified this.

So long as constitutional politics, especially viewed as a binary choice between independence and the status quo, is dominant then all else is obscured. A very different perspective is required to address the very real problems and issues faced by citizens and communities. Sustainable economic growth, improved public services, tackling environmental crises, housing crises, Scotland's shameful record of drug deaths, growing demographic challenges amongst so many other problems, challenges and opportunities requires more than one sphere or level of government and much better coordination and collaboration. There are matters that already wholly come under the responsibility of the Scottish Parliament but the most challenging 'wicked problems' tend to require collaboration across local, devolved and UK central governments. The location of appropriate tools of government is a question that is not best decided in a crude binary choice.

And beyond more powers, other reforms are necessary. The most pressing need is reform at UK central government level and in relations with local government and the wider institutions and processes of local governance, discussed elsewhere in this book. Holyrood itself has added significantly to the scrutiny of government but there is scope for improvement. Institutionally, Holyrood inherited more from Westminster than was expected including much that has undermined good government. Too much was expected of a new electoral system and parliamentary architecture. The much lauded and anticipated consensus never emerged, though that need not be a problem. But manufactured and exaggerated differences could have been limited. First Minister's Questions have proved more relevant to Parliament as theatre and creating easy headlines than serious scrutiny of government. Members have been over-stretched on committees designed to combine roles that are split in the Commons and with far fewer members to fulfil the dual committee functions. The legislative output of Holyrood has given rise to concerns about the quality of laws passed. The Committees have not become the policy initiators initially envisaged nor have they been as effective in scrutinising government as well as hoped. Little attention has been paid to the consequences of increased competences gained over the last quarter century. New powers and responsibilities, most notably the more complex nature of funding and welfare responsibilities, have empowered the Scottish Government rather than the Parliament and have not been matched with new thinking on how the executive/legislature branches should be rebalanced. Early improvements, such as in freedom of information, have been treated as 'job done' rather than requiring regular reviews and revisions.

While the Scottish Parliament in the early days could justifiably be described as a modern Parliament, an improvement on Westminster in its practices and procedures – if not as much as many supporters believed – that is no longer the case. Reforms, albeit modest, have meant that the Commons has leap-frogged Holyrood. The election of Select Committees has helped. There have been proposals to adopt this change in Holyrood from the moment they were introduced in the Commons but there has been little appetite for rebalancing the relationship between executive and legislature in Scotland. If there was a serious interest in a more assertive Parliament, as its founders envisaged, then it would take much more than elected convenors and members of parliamentary committees. The size of the Parliament, especially with Government Ministers drawn from it in such large numbers, precludes effective scrutiny, far less policy initiation.

As well as a neglect of Scotland's internal constitution and the subsuming of policy concerns into a constitutional debate, there has been a lack of focus on wider political changes. The Scottish media has been transformed, in common with global developments. The Scottish press has declined as has the broadcast media while social media has burgeoned. Scotland's local media has been unable to fill the gap, to nurture political interest and involvement. The hoped for democratisation of media has been overshadowed by toxic commentary and elite control. Devolved government, created to provide greater democratic control has been unable to keep up with rapid technological developments. Political parties have been hollowed out. The enthusiasm and engagement that was witnessed during the independence referendum, often enough around much broader debates than Scotland's constitutional status, suggests latent possibilities. The opportunities offered by the surge in SNP membership after the referendum were suppressed by a controlling leadership that simply treated these members as a funding source. The SNP became much more centralised, despite – or perhaps as a response to – the increased membership. The surge in Labour membership under Jeremy Corbyn, also initiated by social movement-style politics, did not result in the lift in membership in Scotland as it had in England perhaps because many who might have joined Corbyn's Labour Party had already joined (and left, disillusioned with party politics) the SNP.

The 'usual suspects' who had dominated access to decision-makers pre-devolution remain dominant post-devolution despite easier access for all. Money and resources have proved vastly more important than geographical proximity even though that proximity has created more opportunities for access for citizens and communities. Holyrood has made valiant efforts to reach out to the wider public but the imbalanced relationship between the Scottish Government and Parliament means power rests emphatically with the former though most attention on access has focused on the latter.

The ideals that inspired support for a Scottish Parliament had largely been negative and defensive. Stopping Thatcherism at the Scottish border helped mobilise support in the 1997 devolution referendum. There has been much progress, many achievements though mostly limited and piecemeal. The independence referendum that started when the SNP won an overall majority dominated Scottish politics for a decade and led debate up a constitutional *cul de sac*. Scottish politics may now be backing out of that *cul de sac* but with little clarity on future directions. The Scottish Parliament was created, predicated on an assumption that Scotland was, if not bolder and more radical than the rest of the UK, then at least less conservative and more progressive. That understanding has been tested and found wanting, but it need not be abandoned as an aspiration. Radical or progressive politics cannot be taken for granted but require ideas, programmes and policies. The emphasis on diverging from policy prescriptions in the rest of the UK has distracted Parliamentarians from the more important divergence required. Scotland needs policies that will help it diverge from past outcomes, its poor record in addressing inequalities, poor economic performance and weakening public services. New thinking is needed that confronts challenges rather than seeks to make political capital out of these challenges in the dismal sparring of party politics.

Just over a century ago, Jimmy Maxton addressed a meeting just before being elected Glasgow Bridgeton's MP at which he argued

Give us our Parliament in Scotland. We will start with no traditions. We will start with ideals. We will start with purpose, with courage.

We have now had that Parliament for a quarter of a century. It's time for the ideals, purpose and courage.

Why Britain Fails, and How It Might Succeed

Salvador Allen Hughes

WRITING IN THE *Daily Telegraph* in 2021, former Labour Prime Minister Gordon Brown claimed that the UK is at risk of becoming a failed state. Brown pointed to the disillusionment felt by citizens across the country with the way the UK is being governed by and in the interests of a London-centric elite. He also highlighted that it is in Scotland where the sentiment of dissatisfaction runs so deep that it threatens to end the very notion of Britain as a polity and called for fundamental political reform to redress these grievances to avoid a slow burn state death by civic asphyxiation.

The existential crisis facing the British state is not confined merely to disaffection with its power-hoarding, overly centralised political system, and its real risk of constitutional fragmentation. After 14 years of dysfunctional Tory Government at Westminster, a decade or more of draconian cuts to public spending and brutal austerity, a hard Brexit, and a botched response to a global pandemic, Britain does feel it may be teetering on the cliff edge of state failure.

This may sound alarmist and hyperbolic to some, but such sentiments are likely underpinned by an innate hubris that a developed Western nation such as the UK could never suffer such a fate. The evidence suggests otherwise.

Failed states share some common characteristics: an inability to provide basic functions of government, such as law enforcement and justice, healthcare, and a stable economy. They also tend to have lost the trust of the people and suffer from high rates of crime, corruption, poverty, civil and industrial unrest, and crumbling infrastructure. Crucially, a failed state is one that can no longer reproduce the conditions for its own existence.

More than one in five people in the UK currently live in poverty. This amounts to 14.4 million people and includes over four million children, the group in society consistently with the highest rates of social deprivation.

While poverty has been increasing, the ability of the state to provide basic support to the poorest and most vulnerable groups in society has been systematically undermined as local government has been eviscerated across the country. Local authority leaders are frequently crying out in exasperation that they simply do not have the resources to perform their basic functions and comply with their statutory duties.

As social need and demand for public services are ever-increasing, resources are simultaneously dwindling, leaving local government squeezed in the middle by a pincer movement of the so-called jaws of doom.

The economy more broadly is extremely unstable, prone to recession, high levels of inflation, and industrial disputes. It is inhospitable to fostering prosperity for the broad base of the population, as the country has lurched from crisis to crisis. To compound the misery of widespread poverty, a headline rate of over 11 per cent inflation in 2022 has fuelled the high cost of living which is driving people, many of them in work, to the brink, relying on the proliferation of food banks for sustenance and casualised labour for income.

The economy is subject to sudden shocks, such as the hike in interest rates following the disastrous Truss mini-budget, making it impossible for businesses and families to plan ahead, destroying the prospects for any sustainable economic growth; instead, we have terminal stagflation.

Since 2022, industrial relations have been at a low not seen in the UK in half a century as workers across different sectors of the economy went on strike, ushering in a new era of discontent. The unrest is not confined to the workplace. Riots rocked England and parts of Northern Ireland in the summer of 2024, fuelled by far-right hate. While not detracting from the overtly racist motives of the riots, it is undeniable that socio-economic conditions in certain parts of the UK make working-class people particularly susceptible to fascist scaremongering from right-wing politicians and a reactionary media. The incarceration of the rioters also highlighted another state failing, namely the crisis in the criminal justice system with prisons at breaking point.

The National Health Service is also in a state of freefall. Still reeling from the global pandemic, the lack of investment over the course of the last 14 years has led to record waiting times, staff shortages, and crumbling infrastructure.

The decimation of the public realm has been coupled with overt corruption at the heart of government in the procurement of PPE contracts during the pandemic, and more recently, accompanied by overt political patronage writ large with the surprise return of former Prime Minister David Cameron to the office of Foreign Secretary after his elevation to the House of Lords.

It is no wonder, then, that trust in UK politics is at rock bottom. According to the pollster, Ipsos Mori, trust in politicians generally has reached its lowest level in 40 years. A mere 9 per cent of the British public say they can trust politicians, dropping to only 2 per cent in the 25–34 age group.

Perhaps more worryingly, trust in the UK's institutions more broadly is also in decline. The UK ranks in the bottom third of countries for confidence in the Government at only 24 per cent of citizens, while perceptions of Parliament are also at an historic low at 23 per cent, far behind our Western European neighbours. Trust in political parties is also at an all-time low at 13 per cent. Meanwhile, support for reform of the UK's institutions is growing as, for example, only 18 per cent of citizens believe that the House of Lords should remain unreformed.

Such is the loss of faith in the UK's institutions that citizens in many parts of the country are rushing to the exit door. In Scotland, in particular, there has been a marked increase in support for independence over the last decade, presently running at around half the electorate. While in Wales, the recently released report of the Independent Commission on the Constitutional Future of Wales makes the case that leaving the UK is a viable option.

Although there is no equivalent desire to break up the Union in England, voter antipathy towards the main Westminster parties, low turnout at elections and anger and distrust toward politicians generally are riding high. The fact that the 2024 General Election saw a mere 52 per cent of UK adults cast their vote, the lowest turnout at a UK parliamentary election since the dawn of universal suffrage, is testament to the rot at the core of our democracy.

The critical levels of distrust in our institutions coupled with the growing support for secession in the Celtic nations points to a state no longer capable of reproducing and sustaining the conditions for its own existence. The failed state, then, no longer seems a hyperbolic metaphor but a realistic possible future.

The UK Government's plan to address many of these deep-seated problems is to promise economic growth. While in opposition, Labour adopted five missions for government and top of the list was its aim to 'kickstart economic growth to secure the highest sustained growth in the G7'.

After winning the 2024 General Election, the new Government outlined its three pillars for achieving economic growth – stability, investment, and reform. Focusing on reform, some of the ideas are promising such as the plans for reform of the planning system, the setting up of a National Wealth Fund, and the creation of GB Energy.

However, while economic growth may be desirable and many of these reforms should be welcomed, there is a basic flaw with the overall plan and the assumptions underlying it. From listening to the Government, one would be forgiven for thinking that they have cracked the fundamental formula for creating economic growth. They have discovered the mathematical equations governing the wave function of the economy, as if they were the modern-day Schrödinger of the social sciences.

This would be to forget, however, that much like quantum physics, economic growth is governed by a fundamental principle of uncertainty. The hard truth is that the question of how a government can achieve growth in their domestic economy is one of life's great mysteries. We should not pretend otherwise, and we should not pin all our hopes on something so ethereal that may never materialise in the real world.

The fetishisation of economic growth *per se* also risks neglecting the more fundamental question: economic growth for whom? It is one thing to achieve successive financial quarters of GDP growth but quite another to control who and where feels the benefits.

What is to stop this newfound economic flowering being concentrated in one geographical region of the UK and the fruits siphoned off, perhaps offshore, for the benefit of the few? The state as currently configured fosters economic extraction for the few; there is no reason to believe this *modus operandi* would change with a new wave of growth, everything else being equal.

GDP growth on its own does not address the highly concentrated patterns of economic ownership in the UK, often in foreign hands. It also does not address the increasingly unequal distribution of wealth or income inequality. This, then, does not sound like the formula for addressing what are much deeper-rooted structural problems facing the UK, restoring trust in institutions, and averting the prospect of state failure.

Perhaps most concerningly of all, the obsession with the mantra of economic growth as a panacea distracts from other proposals for more radical reform which are more likely to bring tangible and material differences to the lives of ordinary people. Specifically, focus should be shifted to devising a programme of radical political and economic reform to effect a fundamental redistribution of power and wealth from the few to the many.

Redistribution of this kind would require increased public spending and investment in the economy of the future, which is currently precluded by the straitjacket of the Government's self-imposed fiscal rules. However, more fundamentally, it would require root and branch reform of the UK's political institutions and state apparatus.

Not only would such a redistribution of power and wealth create a more egalitarian society in the short term, but there is evidence that over the longer term, such fundamental political reform is the most obvious way in which government can also foster economic growth, and more importantly, the right kind of economic growth; a more inclusive form of local and sustainable economic development which really does benefit the broad base of the population, as opposed to merely the ruling elite.

In their landmark 2012 book, *Why Nations Fail*, economists Daron Acemoglu and James A. Robinson argue that the fact that some nations prosper and succeed while other nations struggle with economic development, and even ultimately suffer state failure, is determined by whether the state adopts what they term inclusive political institutions as opposed to extractive political institutions.

Although not free from flaws, the authors make a powerful case demonstrating that a state that allows for a wide diffusion of power across the polity, creating pluralistic political institutions which empower the many, tends to then correspondingly opt for what they term inclusive economic institutions, eschewing more extractive economic models.

The book then postulates that a state with inclusive economic institutions creates the right incentives and economic conditions across the nation to increase overall economic output and productivity by empowering the broad base of the population in the endeavour of creative destruction and technological advancement. As economic growth is unleashed and the wealth of ordinary citizens increases, there is demand for further diffusion of political power which then leads to evermore economic development, creating a positive feedback loop.

The problem in the UK is that the state is extremely centralised, and power concentrated in the hands of the few. Deindustrialisation and the financialisaton of the UK economy since the 1980s, coupled with a rigid neoliberal orthodoxy from the professional managerial class running Westminster, has meant that the UK's strong centralised state has become unconditionally obedient to the interests of finance capital, allowing an extremely extractive economic model to take hold.

The institutional inner logic of the UK political system means there is a bias towards favouring vested interests, further reinforcing the concentration of wealth and power in the hands of the few. This trend can be seen in the fact that over the neoliberal era, the share of UK GDP attributed to wages peaked at 65 per cent in 1975 before falling to around 53 per cent by 2008. Over the same period, the profits share of national income rose steadily. It can also be seen in the 40-year obsession in Westminster with deficit reduction, budget discipline and fiscal rules.

The alliance between the strong centralised state and international capital has created a set of extremely extractive economic institutions. These institutions are in a negative feedback loop with the UK's already extractive political institutions, whereby the more wealth that is extracted by the elite and the more unequal Britain becomes, the more exacting the demands for absolute state obedience and for power to remain centralised.

Unsurprisingly, this suffocates regional development and prevents a wide distribution of wealth and power. By extension, creative destruction and economic growth are stifled, leaving many parts of the country wallowing in a post-industrial economic desert. Power is concentrated in the British state to such a degree that there is then no effective challenge to the death spiral.

To arrest the UK's decline, the negative feedback loop must be broken. This can only be done by implementing fundamental political reform. Although no guarantee, this is the most surefire route government has available to it to foster inclusive and sustained economic growth and development, as well as a more equal society.

While in opposition, Labour appeared to recognise the need to reform the UK's broken state and failing political institutions, when Gordon Brown was asked by the leadership to set up the Commission on the UK's Future. However, since the publication of the 2024 manifesto and subsequent assumption of office, the signs are not encouraging.

For example, abolition of the House of Lords, a relatively uncontroversial proposal that should be considered low hanging fruit has been jettisoned. While we are told it remains a longer-term ambition of the Government, for the foreseeable future, we will have to be content with abolishing the 92 hereditary peerages.

Reform of the House of Lords, however, is merely the tip of the iceberg.

Local government needs to be reinvigorated and to regain its status with new tax powers to ensure it has the means necessary to provide the basic public services that citizens rely on daily. Too much of local government funding comes from central government; more should be raised by the councils themselves.

Councils should also have powers to introduce participatory budgeting for citizens for at least some local government spending to ensure local government is more directly accountable to the local people it serves. Guardrails would be required, however, to ensure that council resources are not diverted away from basic services towards wasteful vanity projects.

The rebuilding of local democracy should include radical devolution to the English regions where combined regional authorities should be furnished with real power over borrowing, spatial and planning issues, transport, housing, health and social care, and education, all backed-up by adequate funding from central government, complemented by additional tax powers.

The existing devolution settlements should also be strengthened. In

Scotland, the Scottish Parliament should be given new tax powers over excise duties as they apply to alcohol and tobacco products as well as betting and gaming levies and the power to introduce a Scottish Wealth Tax. It is also critical that the Scottish Parliament is given full borrowing powers to allow investment in the Scottish economy tailored to the needs north of the border.

Strengthening devolution does not only mean new powers, but also ensuring that the devolved institutions have a voice at the centre. That is why the House of Lords should be replaced with a new fully elected Senate of the Nations and Regions, representing the devolved nations and regions as a counterweight to the House of Commons.

The Senate could be composed of Senators from the nations and regions elected on a degressive proportionality principle, similar to the system used in the German Bundesrat, which would allow Scotland, Wales and the lesser populated English regions to have stronger representation in the UK Parliament. The Senate could retain the revising role of the Lords but could be furnished with new powers including a veto on certain primary legislation. This may include a veto over Bills which fall into areas of devolved legislative competence and/or include a cross-territorial element, or constitutional legislation which alters the relationship between Westminster and the devolved nations and regions. The Senate could also be required to ratify international treaties and appointments to the UK Supreme Court.

The Lower House itself needs major surgery. For a start, proportional representation should be introduced at last to replace the outdated and unrepresentative First Past the Post electoral system. The 2024 General Election underscores how preposterous and untenable the current system has become, leading to the most unrepresentative election result in the history of UK democracy.

Wide-ranging reforms are also required to the way our political parties operate. Not only are the share of the seats won in the House of Commons by the major parties disproportionate to the votes cast by the electorate, but our political parties are not even representative of themselves. The party machines are controlled by hierarchies, enthralled to one or other particular faction, and private donors hold significant sway over their political direction.

This is significant because the political parties, particularly the major parties, are the gatekeepers of our democracy. They control the selection processes to choose parliamentary and local government candidates. It is therefore crucial that regulation of the parties includes ways of making their internal processes more democratic. It may also be preferable to require candidates to undergo open primary selections, or at least to ensure local selection processes are controlled by local party members, to allow a more open and level playing field, and to prevent interference from overzealous party bureaucracies. There may also need to be a greater role for public funding of political parties to limit, or indeed eradicate, the influence of private donors.

Finally, the UK's lack of a codified constitution is no longer sustainable. The complex constitutional relationships within the UK mean the case for having a clear statement of how the state should function is irresistible. The constitution should establish new ways of joint working between the different parts of the country.

The constitution could also enshrine important economic and social rights, including workers' rights, to ensure minimum standards for citizens no matter where they are in the UK, to protect the role and status of trade unions, and to promote industrial democracy.

Many more reforms could be suggested. But the key is that the UK's political and economic institutions need to be more pluralistic, representative and locally accountable to facilitate as wide a diffusion of power and redistribution of wealth across society as possible. This transformation will not only make for a fairer society but may also be the most effective way to stimulate inclusive and sustainable economic growth for the many and to prevent evermore extraction by the few. It may stop Britain failing and help it to succeed.

Losing Our Local

Introduction

Stephen Low

THIS SECTION EXAMINES what at first glance seems to be a paradoxical phenomenon, that the era of devolution has also been an era of centralisation. The capacity to make meaningful decisions locally has been under constant attack since Holyrood was set up. This process has sometimes been carried out under UK or EU instruction, but more often the result of 'made in Scotland' political choices and never seriously contested.

The two chapters in this section examine this process, and the politics underlying it; and then sketch out how we can begin to reverse this trend.

Susan Galloway locates the drive towards centralisation in the 'market-driven politics' dominant throughout the period of devolution so far. She outlines the penetration of outsourcing and contracting of public services through numerous, sometimes far from obvious, but nonetheless disturbing examples.

That a contract culture in public services and 'losing our local' go hand in hand is no surprise. The process of contracting and procuring transforms services into commodities. At which point it is the blunt realities of capitalist enterprise rather than the liberal pieties of market theorists that determine what happens. It is those with the best lawyers rather than intentions for the community who win out.

How else to explain the small number of very big fish swimming in the sea of public contracts who seem to have expertise in everything from school dinners, to running ferries to the Northern Isles: Serco, Capita and Rentokil and, until its implosion, Carillion. Their business specialty isn't delivering services (at which there are many examples of them being horrifically bad), it's spotting where the public sector is making money available and putting as much of it as possible in their shareholders' pockets.

We see a similar process in the third sector where, as local authorities contract for services like care, it is increasingly large, Scotland-wide, rather than local, community-based bodies who win out.

This withdrawal from directly providing public services undermines not just local accountability but democratic accountability overall.

Third-sector organisations which rely on the government for 75–100 per cent of their income cannot call themselves independent in any meaningful sense. This was one estimate of Northern Ireland's third sector made in the 2018 book by Stewart et al, *The state of Northern Ireland and the democratic deficit: Between sectarianism and neoliberalism*.

This concern applies equally to Scotland. Classically there is 'civil society,' that part of society which is separate from the state, but here we have 'civic Scotland,' that part of society grant-funded by the state.

It is this situation of commodified service provision that Dave Watson takes as his starting point in asking how we can start to 'rebuild the public realm'. He points to several roads not taken and outlines proposals whose practicality is matched only by their urgency.

The process of developing a culture that genuinely, rather than rhetorically, empowers communities needs a philosophy of subsidiarity at its centre. It also needs to allow for the idea that people, not markets, should be the decision-makers.

The principal value of Watson's suggestions is that they are not a wish list or an ideal scenario realisable only in the best of all possible worlds. They are instead a set of implementable proposals whose starting point is the situation we find ourselves in and they outline a route to a far better set of arrangements.

A society where we are citizens using services rather than customers seeking contract compliance is one with the capacity for empowerment and equality. That should be our aim. This section shows how much a belief in the efficacy of markets has damaged our capacity to determine the fate of where we live, and how we can start to turn that around.

A Procurement Parliament, Not a Workers' Parliament

Susan Galloway

ARGUABLY THE TWO biggest drivers in setting up Holyrood were a perceived democratic deficit during the Thatcher/Major era, and a wish to avoid the market-driven politics of that time. It is therefore something of a paradox that since its inception the most defining features of Scottish Parliaments have been decreasing democratic control and the cementing of Thatcherite ideology.

This chapter considers how this process has played out in three areas – Housing, Children's Services and Social Care (although there are a wealth of other examples) – and then examines what this tells us about how Scotland has been run in the devolution era.

Regardless of who has been in government over the 25 years of devolution, they have failed to produce any decisive break with neoliberalism. Instead, we have seen an expansion or deepening of the role of market mechanisms across Scottish society generally, and in public services in particular. This of course comes at the expense of local democracy and accountability.

Over the years neoliberalism, as implemented in policy and practice, has been less the Thatcher/Reagan 'combative' model and more the Blair/Clinton 'palliative' model. There have been ameliorations or interventions to lessen the impact of raw market actions, sometimes by insisting on minimum standards. These though are aimed at facilitating market models, not challenging them.

Housing is an obvious example of the drift from social to market values under devolution. The *Housing (Scotland) Act 2001* paved the way for a stock transfer that resulted in six authorities across Scotland losing ownership and control of their entire housing stock. This process was democratic in the sense that tenants had a vote on the matter; it was though made clear that if they chose to say 'no' to transfer, rent rises and a lack of investment were inevitable. There were 'no' votes in Edinburgh, Stirling, Renfrewshire and Highlands; but Glasgow, Scottish Borders, Dumfries & Galloway, Eilean Siar, Argyll & Bute and Inverclyde all voted for transfer.

The central part of the legislation was the extension of the 'right to buy' to Housing Association Tenants, citing a spurious 'need' for a single Scottish Tenancy. The Act did reduce the discount offered to tenants and increased the qualifying period before a tenant had the right to buy. In essence, though, the Act was an extension of Thatcher's flagship policy. Since then, far from Scotland's housing problems ending, they have deepened, although the right to buy has effectively been abolished in a bid to contain the growing crisis. Since 2001 there have been various Acts and initiatives. In 2016, for example, the *Private Housing (Tenancies) (Scotland) Act* made provision for 'Rent Pressure Zones' to provide protections for tenants, but as of October 2024 none have been implemented, possibly because collecting sufficient evidence to submit an application has proved impossible.

The overall impact of the choices made by devolved administrations on housing in Scotland is stark. The private rented sector accounted for 5 per cent of households in 1999 but 13 per cent of households by 2022. In the same period, socially rented households declined from 32 per cent to 23 per cent, and we have a 'housing emergency'. Councils provided a quarter of the country's homes in 1999. Stock transfer, and the mass demolitions that followed, reduced this to 12 per cent. The major response to this is not a decisive expansion of social housing – it is instead an endorsement of landlordism through a 'build to rent' programme.

Devolution has seen both an expansion and development of children's services in and out of school. Here again can be seen a preference for market over social solutions and a willingness to reduce local accountability and particularly the role of local government.

A statutory entitlement to nursery education was introduced for the first time in the early years of devolution in 2002. Prior to this, local authorities had no obligation to provide it, and some didn't. Over the years Early Learning and Childcare (ELC) expanded. Initially it was set at 412.5 hours per year; this has increased in stages to a current level of 1,140 hours per year.

A political choice was made <u>not</u> to deliver this through the public sector by funding local authorities to expand their nursery provision. This mode of delivery would have had the added benefit of achieving collectively bargained pay and conditions, including pensions, for the majority female ELC workforce, ticking multiple 'policy aim' boxes for the Government. Instead, the choice was to expand provision through outsourced, largely private providers renowned for poverty pay. While the introduction and the expansion were delivered under devolution, both the Lab/Lib Dem coalition and SNP opted for the market.

The role of councils as education authorities for schools has been undermined by the retention of the pre-devolution Tory policy of devolved school management. Whilst this had never gone as far as in England, one immediate effect was felt in subjects like music tuition. This now had to be 'bought in' by each individual school. The provision had previously been arranged by local education authorities but is now dependent on the preferences of individual head teachers and has more or less come to an end. (It also made the livelihoods of, eg peripatetic music tutors and the like, much more precarious.)

The sidelining of local authorities has gone further under the SNP. In 2018 the Scottish Government and COSLA adopted the Education Reform – Joint Agreement. This puts in place a framework for greater delegation of decision-making to headteachers including over funding. The Joint Agreement advises that through the Headteachers' Charter, local authorities are to 'empower' headteachers in areas of curriculum, improvement, staffing and funding (much as happened in England in the 1990s). It goes on:

> Local Authorities will continue to be responsible for the Local Authority education budget and the delegation of funding to schools. Headteachers will make decisions on the spending within that delegated budget.

The result is that the role of headteachers has gradually become more like accountants/business managers (as happened in England) which is probably not a role that most would want.

In 2015 the SNP introduced Attainment Challenge funding as part of their number one priority of closing the attainment gap. This was a targeted programme directed at the group of local authorities with the greatest concentrations of multiple deprivation. As part of the Attainment Challenge, Pupil Equity Funding (PEF) was introduced in 2017–2018.

PEF operates by allocating headteachers budgets based on free school meal eligibility, to spend on procuring support for children to raise attainment. Across Scotland it amounts to around £130 million a year.

This is not 'new' money. It is money top-sliced off local authority funding and ring-fenced for this purpose. When PEF was introduced, there had already been a decade of austerity cuts resulting in education authority centralised support services for schools stripped back or cut altogether. These included school liaison or link workers (a supportive link between the school and parents), educational psychology services, family support services, trauma recovery, and intensive social work services organised around schools and nurseries. In place of this collective provision coordinated through local education departments, individual headteachers were awarded PEF funding, which they could use to purchase these services from local providers. PEF created a market and unsurprisingly it has proven to be a highly inefficient way of allocating resources to meet children's needs.

Headteachers are now able to 'buy in' – or rather 'buy back' – services to which their school previously had access before councils were forced to cut back. They have used PEF to 'spot purchase' help for individual pupils or families or to buy the time of a voluntary-sector organisation to provide a school-based service for a target group. This market approach has made things very precarious for voluntary organisations who previously had the relative security of revenue funding from a council to provide a service to all schools in the area, some of which had been in place for many years. Now it is individual head teachers who buy in their service, meaning that it is highly fragmented and insecure.

This fragmentation has had an impact on families as, in some areas, support which had previously been accessible to families across the entire local authority is now confined to individual primary schools whose headteachers choose to buy it. In a report for NSPCC Scotland in 2020 *Challenges from the Frontline – Revisited* I wrote:

> There is evidence that in some local authority areas schools are using PEF as a substitute for services which were previously available to them funded by the council. Three of the original 14 services in this study were established as education-based services, dating from 1998, 2000 and 1987 respectively. All three have closed since 2013 during the time when closing the poverty-related attainment gap became a Scottish Government priority.

Residential care for looked-after children and children with complex needs has become increasingly marketised and outsourced since devolution. A Competition and Markets Authority study in 2022 noted:

> Since 2014/15 there has been a reduction in the share of local authority children's homes in Scotland, and a corresponding increase in the private sector's share of children's homes, whereas the voluntary sector's share has remained relatively stable.

In 2022, 35 per cent of residential childcare places in Scotland were provided by the private sector. The Scottish Government committed to ending the use of for-profit providers following the Independent Care Review report (2020) entitled *The Promise* – but this has not yet been implemented, with private residential childcare operators being paid (at least) £200 million in the intervening period.

The shift away from direct provision and towards marketisation in social care, whether at home or residential pre-dates devolution but, as in the previous examples, devolution has built upon rather than reversed this trend. Indeed, rather than challenging market relations the relevant legislation passed by the Scottish Parliament takes it as a given. Relevant legislation such as the *Community Care and Health (Scotland) Act 2002* and *Procurement Reform (Scotland) Act 2014* assumes a market in health and social care.

It is worth bearing in mind that, although the transfer of care services has generally been justified by a rhetoric of consumer choice and empowerment, this hasn't been the only driver of the shift away from direct provision. In 2014 a joint COSLA and Scottish Government report into the future of residential care was explicit in praising the private and third sector for providing a cheaper alternative to direct provision. In the Scottish Government report *The Future of Residential Care for Older People in Scotland* it was stated:

> We have therefore made considerable progress on the procurement of care in care homes over the last decade. The current mix of provision demonstrates general value for money, especially when private and voluntary sector providers are compared with the cost of in-house provision.

The dominance of market mechanisms in care is therefore not some sort of natural or inevitable phenomenon – it is the result of political choices. The most recent significant example of this was the creation of Integrated Joint Boards following the *Public Bodies (Joint Working) (Scotland) Act 2014*. These bodies direct Council and Health Board spending, and decide what services will be delivered and how – whether through commissioning (from the NHS or council) or procurement (outsourcing). They include a third-sector representative who, although in a non-voting seat, still has a clear business interest.

This has failed to deliver a system fit for purpose. It is fractured, poorly coordinated, with endemic low pay and intractable staff recruitment and retention problems. Residential care has increasingly become dominated by large, for-profit firms, often owned by private equity, whose business model is best described as 'extractive'. The care system was already broken but

Covid made the crisis impossible to ignore. The response from the Scottish Government was not to turn away from market mechanisms to a greater focus on community control. Quite the reverse. It was a legislative proposal seeking not just centralisation, but to get rid of the concept of 'in-house' services entirely.

The *National Care Service (Scotland) Bill* as introduced in 2021, attacked the principle of public sector delivery of public services on a scale unseen in Scotland since the Thatcher era. The legislation, as introduced, proposed to remove statutory responsibility not just for social care but all of social work (including children's and justice services), and community health, away from local government, and where necessary the NHS, and give responsibility to new 'care boards'. These would not deliver services directly but instead use procuring and contracting from the private, voluntary or public sector. The only transfer of ownership envisaged was out of the public sector. Should councils wish to continue providing services, they would have to enter, and be successful in, procurement exercises. That is assuming they would even be allowed to bid, as Section 41 of the Bill allowed care boards to exclude local authorities and health boards even from tendering for contracts.

The financial memorandum issued with the bill was costed on the basis of 75,000 staff being transferred out of local authority employment. It was also explicit how the market mechanism was perceived:

> the market for social care as a whole remains vibrant and stable which will ensure continuity of quality social care provision.

The Scottish Government was finally forced to abandon these plans, which formed the core part of the Bill, following three years of intense opposition. However, the sheer determination with which it pursued them (squandering £28 million of public money in the process) exposed the mindset at the heart of government.

Holyrood has shown that, whatever some might have hoped for, it offers continuity rather than a break with market-driven politics. This has been the case whoever has been in government, Labour/Lib Dem or SNP/ Green. Alongside this, arguably inevitably as democratic accountability is exchanged for contract compliance, has come centralisation.

The principle of local authorities being able to determine what arrangements and provision best meets needs in their area is an important one. The Scottish Parliament's own devolved powers are based upon it. Yet the devolution era has seen the removal of police, fire and water from local services to national services. And while water is still publicly owned, it is being subjected to a process of hollowing out by private contractors.

The politics of devolution have been market driven, but this hasn't been entirely uncontested. Exceptions and ameliorations have been a consistent feature. The 2015 Procurement Guidelines acknowledge that the purchase of care is not the same as the buying of lightbulbs and contracting bodies 'may not use price only or cost only as the sole award criteria.'

The Scottish Government's Fair Work Programme has delivered some tangible benefits since its inception in April 2015. Workers employed by contractors funded by the Scottish Government, either directly or through grants, and those working in care, should be receiving at least the Scottish Living Wage. For many of them of course, that also constitutes a maximum wage.

And there's the rub. These mitigations do prevent the proverbial 'race to the bottom', but that often means settling for second to bottom. These interventions are not made to challenge the commodification of services but to facilitate it. They are not aimed at ensuring publicly delivered public services but rather at making outsourcing acceptable. It bears repeating that the SNP/Green Government put forward a Bill that would have seen public sector organisations, across the entirety of social work, social care and community, involved only if they had been successful in winning contracts (assuming they were allowed to bid).

This, amongst other things, undermines the idea of a public service ethos – and eventually the whole idea of public services, which are forced to be considered not in the round as 'providing care', but as a set of separate and distinct contractual obligations.

For the first 25 years then, the Scottish Parliament has been not the 'workers' parliament' demanded by the STUC in 1972, but a 'procurement parliament'. If we are to make any serious headway in confronting the variety of challenges facing our public services, and communities – that must change.

Rebuilding the Public Realm

Dave Watson

SCOTLAND'S PUBLIC SERVICES are under significant strain, including long NHS waiting lists, under-funded social care, a housing emergency, and concerns over the quality of education. There are also substantial gaps between the policy ambition to tackle Scotland's persistent inequalities and delivery, with inadequate public finance a pivotal barrier to progress. In this chapter, I will focus on the structural reforms necessary to ensure that any new investment effectively addresses the challenges that our public services face.

It is over 13 years since the Christie Commission on the Future Delivery of Public Services reported in 2011. The Commission's key conclusions were that Scotland's public services require comprehensive reform by empowering communities, integrating service provision, preventing negative social outcomes and becoming more efficient. The long-term trends identified around the demand for public services and the impact of demographic change have proved all too accurate. Equally important to the Commission was the growing inequality between the top and the bottom 20 per cent in income, employment, and health outcomes. The consequences of disadvantage impose financial costs on public services, estimated at over 40 per cent of local public service spending. The Commission also recognised the crucial contribution public services made to the Scottish economy and tackled the myth that public services are a drag on economic progress. Sadly, it was all but forgotten during austerity with consequential damage to the Scottish economy.

The Commission identified problems with public service delivery, including fragmented authority and operational duplication, coupled with a top-down approach that designs services for individuals rather than with them. The recommended solutions focused on allowing services and communities to work together to decide what needs to be done, making the best use of all the resources available – taking an integrated, long-term, preventative approach. Leaders should empower staff to actively seek innovative solutions with a strengthened public service ethos and standard training for all staff based on enabling and empowering the lives of people and communities.

Thirteen years on, public service challenges look similar, with the obvious addition of pandemic recovery following austerity economics. Scotland's deep-seated inequalities remain largely untouched, and child poverty has increased. Demographic change has only partially been alleviated by increased migration, and even that is under threat from Brexit and UK Government immigration policies. Austerity has savagely reduced the public service workforce, particularly in local government, forcing staff to abandon the critical Christie prevention approach and revert to the statutory minimum at best.

Integration has been limited, even in the vital area of social care. The idea that all public service organisations operating in a local authority area should view themselves as part of a common framework hasn't happened. The silos that Christie sought to bring down remain very much in place. Instead of a bottom-up approach based on empowerment, we have seen the centralisation of services.

Five years after Christie, I wrote a paper, 'Public Service Reform', for the Reid Foundation. This built on the Christie principles with a call to build integrated public services around recognisable communities, based on the principle of subsidiarity with service delivery at the lowest practical level. I argued that the role of the central government should be to set the strategic direction based on outcomes – rather than trying to direct services from Edinburgh. The government should agree on frameworks that allow the local community to focus on what matters. This should include a public sector ethos and Fair Work principles embodied in a national workforce framework. For example, the single public service worker, on common pay and conditions, suggested by Christie, could minimise organisational and professional barriers and provide confidence for staff to engage in service redesign. We also need to empower public service workers. The risk that something bad will happen because of too little compliance needs to be weighed against the risk of a public servant following the rules to the letter yet failing to add value to those citizens they're meant to serve. The motivation and dedication of Britain's many dedicated public servants is part of what has led to this nation's greatest successes. It can do so again – if leadership is bold enough to let it.

On the financing of public services, the current Labour Government's approach is heavily reliant on economic growth. There is considerable scepticism that this will be enough to repair the damage caused by austerity, even with the welcome Autumn Budget increases.

Rachel Reeves wants Labour to be the government of wealth creation, but that does not explain the reluctance to tax wealth, at least to the same levels as income. Similar challenges exist in Scotland. Scotland's population is projected to continue growing older, and the Scottish Fiscal Commission's Fiscal Sustainability Report 2023 warns that, without action, Scottish Government spending over the next 50 years is projected to exceed estimated funding by an average of 1.7 per cent each year, or £1.5 billion in today's prices.

In his 2022–23 Annual Audit Report, the Auditor General stated:

> The Scottish Government must work with partners to develop a programme of public service reform, including workforce redesign, which balances the short-term financial pressures with the need for longer-term change, recognising that this may require financial investment.

And there is the problem. Public service reform is wheeled out as a solution during a financial crisis, just when the necessary investment is unavailable.

There are other options for increasing taxes to fund investment in public services. The 2023 STUC Report by Howard Reed, *Raising taxes to deliver for Scotland*, outlined measures that could raise £3.7bn. Reform of local taxation is also a better option than another regressive council tax freeze. While there is a case for targeted support for small businesses, the Small Business Bonus is not working and should come with Fair Work conditionality.

Tax Justice Scotland has made a broad-based call for fair tax reform in Scotland. This mirrors other calls for a focus on taxing wealth across the UK. Taxation on income is much higher than on wealth. Much more could also be done to reform tax reliefs and tax dodging. This year, the tax gap between what HMRC is owed and what it collects rose to £36bn.

In his 2019 book, *Plunder of the Commons: A Manifesto for Sharing Public Wealth*, Guy Standing argues that we need to reclaim public wealth. Common land has been captured by private interests from the enclosures to the Highland clearances and modern-day encroachments – leaving most land in the hands of the very few, not the many. Common land today makes up only 7 per cent of Scotland and 5 per cent of the UK. A key recommendation is the establishment of a Commons Fund, sourced by levies on the commercial use or exploitation of the Commons. These levies would also give all citizens a sense of collective ownership, even if it might involve some cost to them personally. Private wealth should be the starting point for the fund as it has increased at the expense of public wealth. Only 4 per cent of tax revenues in the UK come from wealth. Standing proposes a progressive tax on inherited wealth or a general wealth tax, which already exists in several countries.

Other sources of income could include a Land Value Tax, Carbon Levy, Frequent Flyer Levy, Cruise Liner Levy, water use and others. These all have the advantage of encouraging less environmentally damaging activity. A Digital Data Levy could address the use of our personal data by companies adept at tax avoidance, putting a little back into our economy and public services. A similar approach is suggested to intellectual property rights, including ending subsidies for Patents.

Successive administrations have avoided reforming local government finance and council tax. The Council Tax accounts for less than 20 per cent of local government expenditure, leaving communities with little control over their finances. The Commission on Strengthening Local Democracy found that the average for countries where local governments have the equivalent responsibilities to Scotland is between 50 and 60 per cent of the income raised locally. The Burt Report recommended moving towards 50:50 and identified a range of tax powers that should be devolved to councils.

Spending on tackling child poverty is an excellent example of preventative spending. The Scottish Child Payment (SCP) was lauded in recent research:

> The devolution of some social security powers has meant that Scotland has been able to forge a different path, introducing potentially transformative policy reforms.

However, this progress needs to be maintained, with 150 Scottish organisations calling for an increase in the SCP to £30 per week. Spending on education is another excellent example of preventative spending, paying dividends across future generations.

If the pandemic taught us anything, it must be the importance of a genuine safety net for everyone in our society and the weakness of the global economic system. Covid-19 brutally exposed the failings of capitalism and the failure to maintain effective public services. When the pandemic threatened to wreck the livelihoods of those usually comfortable under capitalism, there were pleas for increased state support that had previously been confined to the left. Writing in *The Spectator,* of all journals, Robert Peston quotes a Tory minister saying, 'We'll find ourselves implementing most of Jeremy Corbyn's programme.'

This should be an opportunity to rethink our approach. Instead of a series of ad-hoc measures and bailouts without conditions, we should recognise the value of systems that provide the essentials for everyone. In their 2020 book, *The Case for Universal Basic Services*, Anna Coote and Andrew Percy make a case for expanding the principle of collective, universal service provision. The goal, as they put it, is:

Acting together to help each other, and ourselves, so that everyone has access to three things fundamental to a successful, peaceful, functioning democracy: security, opportunity and participation.

Universal Basic Services builds on what we already have, such as the National Health Service, and expands to meet other essential needs – housing, transport, childcare, adult social care and access to digital information. These are not nice-to-haves but necessities. If anyone who needs them cannot access them, it's not just bad news for those individuals. We all lose in the end. The aim is for sufficiency, not something minimal. Everyone has a right to have their needs met, so there's an underpinning structure of enforceable entitlements. Coote and Percy cost the additional expenditure required for the services proposed at around 4.3 per cent of GDP for a typical OECD country – less than 15 per cent of total government spending in the UK. And that doesn't take account of the savings brought about by economies of scale and a healthier population.

The biggest failure of devolution has been the absence of decentralisation to communities, a vision set out by the Constitutional Convention that has yet to be delivered. Rather than extending the principle of devolution within Scotland, the Scottish Government has retained all the transfers from Westminster and, in addition, has taken away functions from local government. Scottish Ministers direct three-quarters of public spending.

Scotland has some of the largest basic council units in the world, with an average population of 170,000, compared with a European norm of 10,000. Scotland also has the lowest number of elected members per head of population in Europe. England has an average of 2,814 people per councillor, Norway 572 and Denmark 2,216; the average councillor in Scotland looks after 4,155 constituents. A series of commissions and independent reports have highlighted the need to reform local democracy. While they sometimes offer different solutions, a common theme opposes centralisation. Many of these reports have cross-party and civil society support, pointing to a broad consensus on the principle of strengthening local democracy. The aim is not to create more politicians; it is to get more people involved in the governance of our lives. The *Building a New Local Democracy in Scotland* Declaration has brought together a broad coalition of academics, trade unionists, former council leaders and journalists to make the case for change.

Austerity has undermined many of the local institutions that bind our communities together. Cuts to our libraries, community learning, youth work, day centres, and grants to voluntary organisations have all weakened local communities. These cuts adversely and acutely impact the most disadvantaged individuals, communities, and groups. That is why social infrastructure is vitally important to strong communities. Social infrastructure relates to the physical conditions that determine whether personal relationships can flourish. When social infrastructure is robust, it fosters contact, mutual support, and collaboration among friends and neighbours. When degraded, it inhibits social activity, leaving families and individuals to fend for themselves. In *Building Stronger Communities*, a 2020 paper for the Reid Foundation, I examined a wide range of initiatives that can strengthen social infrastructure, including suitable housing, libraries, leisure facilities, voluntary organisations, community ownership and the role of planning. Social media can be part of social infrastructure, but it depends on connectivity, which can be limited and unequal in many communities.

A strong local economy is an essential element of strong communities. Scotland's high streets and town centres struggled even before the pandemic, with five stores closing a week. We must rethink our town centres as places where people live and work, not just shop, although that will remain important. Community Wealth Building should be at the core of the measures needed to rebuild local economies based on wellbeing and inclusion.

Stronger communities must also be sustainable, based on more local (mainly food) production, community energy, developing a sharing economy, better public transport and support for active travel. Place also impacts health and wellbeing and contributes to creating or reducing inequalities. Sufficient social infrastructure helps tackle isolation and improves physical and mental health. This includes designing communities and creating integrated local health and care services.

Providing better services is, however, not enough to create stronger communities; citizens must also be actively engaged. So, local democracy should sit alongside measures to decentralise powers and democratise the economy. A fairer Scotland is one where we care about each other, where people can pool their resources, demand accountability, build institutions and influence the decisions that affect them. Local integrated services should be based around community hubs in recognisable communities of place. The pandemic has highlighted the importance of local services and the workers who deliver them – we should 'Build Back Better' based on the principle of subsidiarity.

Some 200 public bodies administer Scotland's public services. Most of these are run by boards that make the critical decisions on most public spending in our country. This means we should pay close attention to the governance of public boards. In recent years, we have been presented with multiple examples of poor governance, including the Scottish Police

Authority, Calmac, colleges, and the Water Industry Commission. Workforce representation can also provide a real challenge. The Fair Work Convention report recommended a worker representative on every Scottish public body. Some have non-executive directors with a workforce interest. While these appointments offer an expertise that might otherwise be ignored, they are not a substitute for an employee director. However, such directors must be supported and accountable; otherwise, they can become isolated and less effective.

The starting point must be subsidiarity, building integrated public services from the bottom up and sharing where appropriate. Central government should set the strategic direction based on outcomes rather than trying to direct services from Edinburgh. However, a country the size of Scotland cannot justify duplication and difference for its own sake. Therefore, we need public service frameworks that allow local services to focus on what matters to achieve positive outcomes. Even where decentralisation is not viable, services should still be required to cooperate locally more effectively than currently. The somewhat loose duties placed on quangos to collaborate in community planning have no effective teeth. Scotland is one of the most centralised states in Europe. Until we address this centralisation of power, the devolution project will remain unfinished.

Who Controls the Scottish Economy?

Introduction

Vince Mills

THE 1975 *Red Paper on Scotland* made a powerful case that unless there was a challenge to the dominance of global market forces, Scotland was and would remain in a weak economic position, despite the increasing flows of North Sea oil. As Gordon Brown put it in his introduction:

> ...the Scottish economy is perhaps more subject to the influence of multinationals than any other similar industrial country. Consequently the economy is not only... an unstable one, one of the first to suffer and the last to recover in times of depression but also dependently subordinate to the international market, with an increasingly distorted and artificial division of labour, compounded by the massive export of capital... even *The Business Scotland* was moved to write, recently: 'Scotland in calling for jobs at any price for the past ten years has been engaged in turning its economy into one akin to that of a colony, i.e. one with a high level of external control, absentee decision makers and subsidiary technology.

That was 50 years ago and since then, it has got worse. In this section, drawing on his comprehensive work *The State of Capitalism,* Costas Lapavitsas outlines why those deep structural problems of capitalism outlined by Brown in 1975 have deepened, especially in the wake of the financial crash of 2007–8 – a crisis hastened by the then Chancellor, Gordon Brown's, desire for 'light touch' regulation.

The crisis, which was created mainly through an excess of speculation by unregulated banks, was 'resolved' in the core capitalist countries by state intervention – a bailout – leading to a massive expansion of the public debt.

In the UK, the incoming Conservative/Lib Dem coalition in 2010 denied the real nature of the problem, pointed their fingers at 'unaffordable' public expenditure under the previous Labour Government, and used it as an excuse to introduce austerity.

As Costas Lapavitsas also points out, this occurred while financialisation of the economy steadily increased, including the rise of 'shadow banking'

– organisations that provide services similar to traditional banks but are not covered by tight regulations. In an age of austerity these functioned, among other things, to increase private household debt, especially as social housing became harder to access. Meanwhile multinationals, primarily, but not exclusively from the United States, Europe and Japan extended their reach, establishing global production chains in which they had a controlling interest while domestic productive capacity in core capitalist countries declined.

Richard Leonard assesses this continued externalisation of Scotland's economy. He points out that it has intensified and that the creation of the Scottish Parliament has had no significant impact on impeding this process. Indeed, under the SNP, attracting foreign direct investment has remained a priority. This includes newer sectors like renewable energy. These too are dominated by multinationals whose headquarters are overseas. Furthermore, as the most recent leasing of ScotWind demonstrates, if anything, the Scottish Government is accelerating the sell-off of Scottish energy assets to private corporations and overseas state-owned utilities.

Nor does he believe that the new Labour government's intention to create Great British Energy, to be located in Aberdeen, will reverse this process. Instead, he fears its principal aims will be offering financial assistance, grants, loans and share acquisitions to private sector providers. Nevertheless, he is at pains to insist on the continued importance of manufacturing because, as recently as 2023, it accounted for 53 per cent of the value of all Scotland's international exports. Leonard wrote his article before the fate of the Petrochemical plant in Grangemouth had been revealed. No doubt he would have added that to the long list of lost economic opportunities in Scotland since the first Red Paper of 1975.

Sara Cowan correctly takes that 1975 publication to task, not only for failing to have any female authors, but also, hardly surprisingly given that omission, failing to consider the economic impacts of the economy on women.

Cowan rectifies that, arguing that today there needs to be rapid change in economic policy to tackle the ingrained inequality and poverty, that women suffer. Central to that policy shift, Cowan argues, is care, which is essential for a successful economy. Her analysis is based on a consideration of recent evidence on women's economic position, as well as an assessment of the role of care both in women's position in the labour market and the economy more widely.

All three authors conclude by setting an agenda for the left that is demanding but optimistic. Cowan argues that building an economy that works for women and men is possible but that we must value and invest in care. Such an economy will be one that works better for everybody.

Leonard believes that we can transform our economy, including achieving a net zero future, but not if we are colonised by multinational corporations, global capital and financial markets. He recognises that this requires a movement inside the trade unions and in the wider society struggling for that change.

Very much in tune with both of these, Lapavitsas acknowledges that we need to take a radical approach to reverse the damage done through decades of globalised and financialised capitalism. This is only possible if we challenge the power of the elite that has grown rich on the politics of the last five decades. For him, and for all of us, this is surely the central social and political task of our time.

Groping For a Way Out of the Mire – A World View of the Economy

Costas Lapavitsas

THE GREAT CRISIS of 2007–9 was a landmark event for the world economy, as is acknowledged even by mainstream economists. In the long history of capitalism, crises of that magnitude have often acted as catalysts for a new phase of economic activity. But the crisis of 2007–9 did nothing of the sort. It merely signalled the peak of financialisation and globalisation of capitalism that began in the late 1970s.

The period that followed is an interregnum, a time during which the forces of financialisation and globalisation no longer possess their previous vigour, but no comparable forces are emerging to take their place. Mature economies – especially in Europe – are effectively in a mire. This is the appropriate context in which to discuss current developments in economic activity and policy, including in the UK.

In this respect, the emergence of the so-called 'modern supply-side economics' is highly revealing. It seems to be an approach to policy that puts a priority on improving the supply and skills of labour, the quality of public infrastructure, and the protection of the environment. It was promoted by the Biden Administration in the USA in the 2020s and was used to justify the adoption of industrial policy. It also seems to have influenced the incoming British Labour Government in 2024.

For our purposes, the importance of 'modern supply-side economics' does not lie in the measures and policies it proposes, but rather in the recognition that contemporary capitalism is ailing primarily on the side of supply, or more accurately, of production.

For roughly a decade after the Great Crisis, economic policy at the core of the world economy was in the grip of austerity. The fiscal policies of several governments – most notably in the UK under the Tories – restricted expenditure and raised taxes, thereby compressing aggregate demand. The prevalent perception was that austerity would 'cleanse' the economy, thus putting it on a path of virtuous growth. In practice, austerity exacerbated economic and social problems, and consequently attracted severe criticism, primarily from the left.

As the interregnum unfolded, however, and particularly following the shock of the pandemic crisis of 2020-1, it became clear that austerity, profoundly harmful as it is, is not the only source of trouble. The malaise of contemporary capitalism goes deeper and lies in production, the site where value and profit are produced.

The financialisation and globalisation of capitalism since the late 1970s are inextricably linked to the rise of huge enterprises dominating domestic economies and dictating the patterns of international trade, investment, and finance. The concentration of market and other power by such enterprises certainly varies among core countries; it seems, for instance, to be greater in the USA than in Europe. But there is little doubt that gigantic multinationals – which used to be called monopolies – rule the roost domestically and internationally.

A characteristic development accompanying the rise of these enormous capitalist concentrations is the relative decline of domestic productive capacity in core countries – USA, Canada, UK, Germany, France, Italy and Japan – vividly apparent in manufacturing and industry. Its counterpart is the rise of independent centres of capitalist accumulation away from the historic core, most notably in China, the contemporary 'workshop of the world'.

This development is in large part the result of sustained state intervention in countries other than in the core. But it was also fostered by the export of capital from the core, particularly of productive capital. By exporting capital, the multinationals established global production chains in which they typically hold dominant positions, thereby shifting manufacturing and industrial capacity across borders. Inevitably, international trade also grew greatly as products were transacted within production chains.

The gist of the globalisation of capitalism consists precisely in the expansion of production across borders and the concomitant growth of commerce. In historical terms, it represents the accelerated internationalisation of productive capital, a striking feature of our times.

Equally characteristic of the period since the late 1970s is the rise of enormous financial corporations underpinning the preponderance of the financial sector in core economies. The financial sector also expanded greatly in peripheral economies since the late 1990s. The rise of huge banks and other financial institutions reflects the financialisation of capitalism during this period, a process marked by three crucial features.

First, globally active corporations have financialised in the specific sense that they hold vast amounts of liquid money capital, which they do not invest productively. Nonetheless, they regularly deploy a broad array of financial techniques and utilise the money capital they hold to ensure the accrual of profits to their shareholders.

Second, financial institutions have relatively less scope for lending to large corporations, particularly since the latter are not short of liquid funds. Consequently, financial institutions seek profits in other ways, including transacting in financial markets and lending to households. In the decades of financialisation this trend gave rise to a vast array of 'shadow banks', distinct from commercial banks. The 'shadow banks' have proved important to the trajectory of core economies during the interregnum.

Third, households have become heavily implicated in finance, through both loans (mortgages and unsecured consumer loans) and assets (pension policies, deposits, etc). Their income and wealth have become a field of profit making for financial institutions, giving rise to direct financial expropriation.

Financial institutions were able to transact in real time across the globe, also bringing developing countries into the financial fold. The result was the strengthening of financialisation among core countries and the emergence of subordinate financialisation in peripheral countries, the latter being derivative of the former.

These extraordinary and complex tendencies peaked in the Great Crisis of 2007–9. What followed was a decade and a half of floundering for both core and periphery, with the UK as one of the worst cases.

It is important to note that all the changes instrumental to the globalisation and financialisation of capitalism have required the conscious intervention of the state.

Thus, globalisation required a raft of international agreements and treaties to manage investment and trade flows. They are continually supervised by state-created institutions which ultimately protect the interests of the great multinationals. Similarly, financialisation required systematic state intervention to divert mass savings and the spare funds of corporations to the open financial markets. It also required legislation to free the flows of capital across borders, while introducing some regulatory measures to protect financial institutions from their own excesses. Not least, financialisation required a host of institutions to oversee global capital flows and manage international debts to protect lenders.

The state has been the indispensable pillar of both globalisation and financialisation. But it has performed this role under the misleading guise of neoliberalism, an ideology which purportedly advocates the shrinking of the state in the face of the market. Not for the first time in the history of capitalism what was officially promulgated was the opposite of what took place in practice.

Still, the economic power that the state currently holds in core countries is plainly enormous. This power derives primarily from command over the money used domestically and internationally.

The issuing of fiat money by the central bank is the ultimate pillar of both globalisation and financialisation. Fiat money is government-issued currency not backed by a physical commodity such as gold or silver. Fiat money has made it possible for the state to rescue core economies in times of crisis and allowed the interregnum to continue for a decade and a half. In the case of the USA, furthermore, the power of the Federal Reserve to issue fiat dollars is the mainstay of global US economic, political, and even military power.

The monetary power of the state is not, however, sufficient to jolt core economies in a new historic direction. The chief weakness of the interregnum lies on the side of supply, or production, and thus requires far more decisive steps than simply manipulating money.

In summary terms, capitalist enterprises compete by producing more cheaply than others, which implies striving to lower costs per unit of output. Lower costs could obviously be attained by somehow paying less for labour (either by lowering wages or making workers work longer for the same wage), energy, raw materials, and so on. However, the systematic way for costs to be lowered is to raise the productivity of labour. For that, it is necessary to invest in productive capacity, while taking advantage of the latest technology. This is what Marxist political economy would term the 'internal mechanism'.

By raising productivity, the 'internal mechanism' also raises the profitability of the investing enterprise. But as the productive advance spreads across the economy, it makes the burden of investment heavier for every unit of output, thus undermining profitability. There is no escape from these contradictory pressures deeply engrained in capitalist production.

The trouble with production in core countries – particularly sharp in the interregnum – is that the productivity of labour has been rising very slowly. In some instances, as in the UK, it has not risen practically at all since the Great Crisis of 2007–9. A fundamental reason for the weak growth of productivity is that investment in fixed capital has been historically low.

Thus, we come full circle. Relatively low investment, including by large corporations, is the most striking feature of core countries during the period of globalisation and financialisation. Low investment is a vital factor behind poor productivity growth, thereby disrupting the 'internal mechanism'. The more that globalisation and financialisation spread, the greater the disruption.

One response was inevitably to drive wages down, a tendency that has marked the entire period, especially in the USA. But it is obvious that resorting to lower wages is not nearly as systematic as raising the productivity of labour. Moreover, over time it creates vast inequality, and the resulting social tensions become explosive.

Another response was to rely on an 'external mechanism', that is, to import commodities that lower the cost of production. That has also marked the period of globalisation and financialisation as cheap goods from China and elsewhere have helped keep costs low, including real wages. But relying on cheap imports is also problematic over time as it tends to contribute to deficits on the current account. Moreover, it increases reliance on global production chains, which stretch over enormous geographical areas and are thereby precarious, not even mentioning their adverse environmental effects.

To make matters worse, China, which has engaged in gigantic investment for a long time, chalking up rapid productivity growth, boosting profitability, and escalating competitive strength, has also hit a plateau in the period after the Great Crisis. The so-called 'New Normal' is marked by lower growth and lower profitability. In the case of China, the fundamental reason appears to be the opposite of core countries, namely excessive investment lowering its own efficiency in bringing down costs.

To be more specific, currently China still invests double the proportion of its GDP compared to most core countries. The beneficial impact of this extraordinary investment on labour productivity has declined significantly with the passage of time, and so has profitability. The country needs a more rational allocation of its resources, lowering investment as a proportion of GDP and allowing Chinese workers to enjoy more of the fruits of their own labour by reducing inequality. But the economic, social, and political risks in bringing this change about are manifestly enormous.

The crisis of 2007–9 hit the large commercial banks of the USA, the UK, France and Germany particularly hard. They were all heavily involved in the US real estate bubble of 2001–6, channelling funds into the financial markets for securitised mortgages and speculating on capital gains.

The bubble was also a time of strong growth for the previously mentioned 'shadow banks'. This is an envelope term that captures a wide array of financial institutions that differ considerably among themselves but have one thing in common: unlike commercial banks, they do not create money by making loans and accepting deposits.

When the crisis burst out, core states intervened and rescued big banks, partly by providing capital out of tax receipts, and partly by supplying liquidity as central banks created large volumes of fiat money. But the aftermath of the crisis was severe for big banks as they had made large losses and as regulatory changes were brought in to limit their room for speculation, especially in the USA with the so-called 'Volcker rule' limiting the activities of banks in the securities markets. The result was that 'shadow banks' acquired a greatly expanded scope for their operations.

Regulatory room aside, a further factor that encouraged the growth of 'shadow banks' was sustained economic intervention by core states through central banks. As growth rates weakened in the 2010s, core states undertook so-called 'Quantitative Easing', a policy that basically amounts to creating vast volumes of fiat money used in part to purchase greatly expanded government debt. The interregnum is thus marked by vastly escalating public debt for core countries together with floods of fiat money created by enormously enlarged central banks.

In this environment, and as commercial banks found themselves relatively constrained, 'shadow banks' grew significantly. They are primarily investment funds that hold huge portfolios of securities – both public and private – and operate globally.

Such funds, by definition, benefit from constantly rising stock markets, and thus have an inbuilt incentive to expand the assets they hold. Consequently, they rely on abundant and cheap liquidity to augment and manage their portfolios in the most profitable way. The floods of fiat money created by central banks, coupled with the sustained policy focus of monetary authorities to prevent heavy falls of stock prices, proved extremely propitious to 'shadow bank' growth.

The result is that three of these gigantic funds – Blackrock, State Street, and Vanguard – currently hold an extraordinary proportion of the entire equity capital of the USA, perhaps as much as 50 per cent.

Financialisation did not go away, even if it peaked in 2007–9. As the interregnum unfolded, its centre of gravity shifted toward 'shadow' financial institutions, which are even further removed from production than large commercial banks. The result of this shift became apparent when the pandemic crisis struck.

The shock of 2020 was gigantic as entire sectors were forced to close to deal with the epidemic, while global production chains were severely disrupted. Faced with collapsing economies, core states did not repeat the foolish austerity practices of the 2010s. They intervened in the economy by, first, creating even more gigantic volumes of fiat money and, second, temporarily encouraging more public spending.

The outcome was a further escalation of public debt in the early 2020s but that was far from the main problem of core states. Given the underlying weakness of production, the boost delivered to aggregate demand through money creation and public spending resulted in a sharp jump of inflation for the first time since the late 1970s.

Inflation is a mortal threat to financialised capitalism since it destroys the value of loaned capital. As inflation escalated, core states took action to throttle it, which basically meant substantially raising interest rates. The cost of confronting inflation was thus borne mostly by working people, who lost out as real wages fell due to price increases and as the cost of mortgages escalated. The social pressures were particularly severe in the UK, giving rise to the 'cost of living crisis'.

Even more significant, however, was the realisation that creating huge volumes of fiat money and manipulating aggregate demand were no longer capable of dealing with the problems of the interregnum. Capitalist weakness lay with supply.

This weakness in production is why 'modern supply-side economics' began to gain purchase among core governments. The Labour Chancellor, Rachel Reeves, declared herself a believer in 'securonomics', a British variant of the US approach. In Britain this is best understood as a promise to build an economy that provides security for working people by revitalising the National Health Service, boosting house building, improving transport, and providing clean energy. These require increases in fiscal expenditure.

Reeves, however, intends to be 'fiscally prudent': money would only be borrowed to invest, and public debt should fall. She spent her first months as Chancellor severely restraining even the modest promises that Labour had made before the election, limiting the size of both the projected National Wealth Fund, which aims to improve infrastructure, and the resources of the planned Great British Energy.

The budget that Reeves eventually presented in October 2024 was hailed as a bold move to tackle UK economic weaknesses. In truth, it was no more than a modest attempt to deal with the disaster bequeathed by 14 years of Tory rule. Reeves increased annual public spending by nearly £70 billion for the next five years, of which one-third will be investment. The bulk of the expenditure will go to the NHS and education.

To do this, Reeves changed the fiscal rules, first, by allowing borrowing to finance some current expenditure and, second, by altering the definition of (and thus reducing) net public debt. Half of the spending will be funded by moderate tax increases on businesses, mostly raising employers' National Insurance Contributions from 13.8 per cent to 15 per cent, and by imposing some small increases on capital gains. The other half will come from borrowing.

Reeves's budget will probably boost growth for one or two years, allowing the stagnant UK economy to breathe. But there is no reason to believe it is a sea change for Britain. The profound weakness of the supply side in the UK is inextricably linked to the country's appalling performance in productivity. This is, first and foremost, the result of weak private investment together with a dearth of public investment. Reeves's modest increase in public investment, welcome as it is, barely begins to scratch the surface.

Instead, Reeves would need to undertake serious public investment as a first step, not possible if fiscal rules remain 'prudent'. The Labour Government would also need to take into public ownership broad swathes of public utilities, including transport, to drive up productivity, not private profit.

It would also mean improving the provision of credit and finance to the productive sector by controlling the activities of the City of London and creating effective public financial institutions. Finally, it would require urgent steps to improve real wages and reduce the appalling inequalities that ravage the supply of labour power in the UK.

The production side of the UK economy is one of the worst among the core countries of the world economy. Radical steps would be necessary to reverse the damage wrought by decades of globalisation and financialisation. Such steps would, in turn, require challenging the power of the elite that has benefitted greatly from the policies of the last four decades and more. As long as that power remains intact, the UK and other core countries will continue to grope blindly for a way out of the interregnum. This is one of the main social and political tasks of the present time.

Controlling our Economy

Richard Leonard

HALF A CENTURY ago, John Firn wrote his seminal essay on the Scottish economy in *The Red Paper on Scotland* 1975, highlighting the extent and the nature of external control of Scotland's manufacturing industry.

He pointed to the dominance of the branch plant and the gradual erosion of decision-making from the Scottish economy resulting in major decisions on investment, sales and purchasing being made elsewhere.

He warned that the supply chain was externalised too, with many of the branches and subsidiaries located inside Scotland purchasing most of their requirements from outside Scotland. With the result that although these companies sold most of their output in Scotland, the parent company benefitted in the form of interest, profits and dividends.

Nor were there any long-term benefits, through external investment in innovation or skills, because there was a very low research and development component associated with the 'branch plant' economy. His conclusion was stark:

> ...it is becoming difficult to talk meaningfully of a distinct 'Scottish Economy' except in a strict geographical sense.

Despite this warning, much governmental economic intervention has been designed to win globally mobile capital investment, rather than develop the indigenous business and manufacturing base. There has been scant interest in a more equal distribution of wealth and power in Scotland's economy.

Even in the devolution era, which now makes up over half of the intervening years since the first *Red Paper* was published, nothing much has changed. In fact, if anything, under the SNP there has been a renewed emphasis on attracting foreign direct investment.

Even Scotland's emerging and growing sectors, like renewable energy, are dominated by overseas-headquartered multinationals: whether it's the redevelopment of the fabrication yards at Nigg Bay and Ardersier in the Highlands or the most recent ScotWind leasing round, which saw overseas state-owned utilities and private corporations snapping up our offshore wind development rights.

It is as if we have learnt nothing from history. Exactly 50 years on, we are simply repeating the same mistakes that created the conditions which led to the squandering of the enormous wealth generated by North Sea oil and gas exploration and production.

Back in 1975, the Labour Government established the publicly owned British National Oil Corporation, headquartered in Glasgow. It was charged with establishing majority state participation in all future oil licences, only for it to be privatised and sold off in the Thatcher neoliberal experiment of the 1980s. In turn, oil and gas revenues were wasted to fund millions on the dole on the one hand and to cut taxes for the wealthiest on the other.

Half a century later, today's Labour Government has created Great British Energy, headquartered in Aberdeen. It is to be tasked, we are told, with the production, distribution, storage and supply of clean energy. But this includes unsafe and uneconomic nuclear options. In reality, GB Energy will be primarily focused on offering financial assistance, grants, loans and share acquisitions to private sector providers. It is more of an investment vehicle in the service of the extractive profit and dividend sector than a publicly owned energy producer or distributor.

This must also be seen in the wider Scottish economic context where there is no industrial strategy, no distinctively Scottish approach, no plan for jobs, no just transition, no, in the enduring words of John Firn, 'long-term dynamic economic strategy.'

The result is that a redistribution of power and wealth has taken place, but it has gone in precisely the wrong direction. We have witnessed a growing concentration of economic wealth and power in fewer and fewer hands with the result that real inequality is rising.

Table 1 provides a snapshot of the changes in employment in the Scottish economy over the last half a century.

Table 1: Employment (thousands) by sector, all enterprises

	1973	2003	2023
AG & FISHERIES	50	38	27
MANUFACTURING	676	263	185
CONSTRUCTION	170	122	156
MINING, GAS, WATER	62	42	61
DISTN, HOTELS, REST	242	546	273
OTHER SERVICES	883	1,139	1,058
TOTAL	2,084	2,278	2,110

The picture of economic ownership in Scotland that emerges is captured in Table 2. It illustrates the low levels of local control and ownership in larger enterprises in all sectors of the Scottish economy.

Table 2: Employment in 250+ Employees by ownership (all sectors) 2023

SCOTTISH	REST OF UK	ABROAD	TOTAL
344,580	273,010	313,840	931,430
37%	29%	34%	100%

Table 3 tracks what has happened to manufacturing jobs over time: both a catastrophic collapse in numbers, and a striking hollowing out of the rest-of-UK-owned manufacturing base.

Table 3: Employment by ownership in Manufacturing (registered enterprises only)

	SCOTTISH	REST OF UK	ABROAD	TOTAL
1973	243,440 (41%)	235,050 (40%)	112,110 (19%)	590,700
2003	148,390 (58%)	49,210 (19%)	64,770 (23%)	255,370
2023	99,120 (56%)	16,460 (9%)	61,570 (35%)	177,160

If we break down the manufacturing sector further (see Table 4), we find that by 2023 employers with over 250 workers employed almost half (48 per cent) of all employees. They also generated over 60 per cent of turnover in Scotland's manufacturing base. This is despite the fact that these employers constituted less than 3 per cent of the number of registered enterprises.

Table 4: Employment in 250+ employees by ownership (Manufacturing) 2023

SCOTTISH	REST OF UK	ABROAD	TOTAL
26,390 (31%)	14,250 (17%)	43,650 (52%)	84,300

Fifty years on from Firn's original analysis manufacturing still matters because even in 2023 it accounted for 53 per cent of the value of all Scotland's international exports. By comparison, financial services accounted for just 6 per cent by value of international exports.

It must be noted that Scotland's businesses export one and a half times more to the rest of the UK (worth £48.5 billion) than is sold to the whole of the rest of the world put together (worth £31.3 billion). And, by contrast with its international export performance, financial services account for 19 per cent of all of Scotland's rest of UK export earnings.

Overall, Scotland's international export base is way too narrow: just 60 firms account for 50 per cent of Scotland's total exports. And the 'research and development component' remains very low.

Across the UK research and development is heavily focused on the so-called Golden Triangle of London, Oxford and Cambridge. In 2022, 56.7 per cent of all UK research and development expenditure went to the East of England, the South East and London regions combined. That's ten times more than the level of research and development spent in Scotland which made up 5.5 per cent of the UK total.

But the level is not just low compared to the Golden Triangle. Scotland's record on business research and development places it seventh out of 12 UK nations and regions as measured by spending, eighth as measured by employment generated, and eighth equal in the amount claimed in research and development tax credits.

And as far as overall private business investment in Scotland is concerned, at £19.5 billion this equates to 9.8 per cent of Scotland's GDP. For the UK as a whole, it is £269 billion equivalent to over 10 per cent of GDP (2023). The average ratio in G7 countries is nearly twice this level at 18 per cent. And one of the reasons for that disparity is in plain sight.

After over a decade of austerity while wages and salaries as a share of GDP have flatlined, at around 49 per cent, dividend payments to shareholders have continued to rise, hitting record levels in 2023, with £86.7 billion paid out – a jump of 66.6 per cent (in nominal terms) compared to a decade before (2013). So instead of profits patiently re-invested in business development they are disbursed to impatient share owners.

No wonder a Scottish Government report in 2022, the *Wealth and Assets Survey, 2018–20*, found that:

> Wealth Inequality was more severe than income inequality: the 2% of households with the highest incomes had 9% of all income, while the wealthiest 2% of households had 18% of all wealth.

Over the last decade and a half, the wealth of the richest has continued to grow by four to five times that of the bottom 50 per cent.

It doesn't have to be this way. There are alternatives to be found in democratic socialism, a new economic vision not one based on a gradual re-ordering of capitalism, which nibbles at it, but one founded on a series of scaled reforms: land reform, industrial reform, democratic reform in the economy. There can be a firm rejection of the market or growthism based on social and environmental justice and the understanding that in order to change society we have to change power relations in the economy. What we need are not just alternatives within the system, but alternatives to the system. After all, if socialism means anything it is surely the extension of democracy into the economic as well as political system.

As we have seen, the commanding heights of the Scottish economy are now predominantly externally owned and controlled. There is an investment gap – both public and private – and economic decline, deindustrialisation and stagnation. And there is a huge imbalance: not only in ownership and so power, but in what is produced, and how it is produced.

That's why we must look at a synthesis of ideas and strategies: from active government intervention and public ownership, to realising the potential of private and public sector pension funds. From revitalised local government and an extension of municipal ownership to an enhanced role for trade unions both in the workplace and in formulating a Scottish economic plan.

It means substantially greater support for self-management and co-operatives: particularly workers' co-operatives.

It will entail reviewing the terms of reference and the governance and resourcing of investment institutions like the Scottish National Investment Bank which in its early years has poured money into tax avoidance schemes for the wealthy, rather than sticking to an unrelenting focus on bridging the investment gap for indigenous businesses, especially in our manufacturing base.

The Investment Bank's primary role must be to ensure that new technologies which are invented here, are then developed, engineered, manufactured and exported from here, so that we secure the jobs dividend.

It is about putting in place practical support for physical but also social infrastructure for the development of industrial clusters to reap the benefits of shared services and knowledge exchange, and creating a changed culture of inter-company co-operation in areas like marketing, training, finance and design.

Public ownership also has an important role to play. Too many strategic national assets including our energy systems, transport networks, and infrastructure rest solely in private hands. Privatisation and outsourcing leaves behind it a trail of lost opportunities, wasted chances and profits extracted.

It is clear that we need an industrial strategy that incorporates a renewed role for democratic, strategic economic planning in the corporate economy. So that, in place of global corporations nesting in the realm of political decision-making, the Government instead provides economic leadership and drives agreements on investment, research and development and jobs that follow.

In *The Red Paper 2005* 20 years ago I pointed out that the emergent renewable energy sector provided an opportunity to lead the manufacturing renaissance of Scotland, and that we had a global advantage because of our vast experience of maritime engineering applications over 30 years in the North Sea.

Much ground has since been lost, years have been wasted, but we need now to instigate public interventions, through an active state to secure this transition. That means a break from the costly over-reliance on external ownership, the branch plant model, which leads inevitably to the extraction of wealth and capital and so of profits and dividends from the Scottish economy.

This could be through the vehicle of GB Energy with a new purpose, alongside a reformed and properly resourced Scottish National Investment Bank so that it is working to secure democratically owned, locally controlled innovation and enterprise.

The way forward is about unleashing transformative change from below rather than simply relying on a command-style top-down approach. It means bringing in, not shutting out, the experience and expertise of workers.

That will include a community wealth building dimension. The value of Scottish public procurement alone is worth £11 billion. This should be used to boost SMEs and local supply chains instead of multinational corporations.

There is also a case for looking again at the wage earners fund model, first introduced in Sweden in the 1970s as part of the Meidner Plan, which could convert privately owned enterprise to indigenously and worker owned businesses.

This would boost the diversity, inclusivity and democracy of ownership.

A worker ownership fund and a Marcora-style law which would bestow on workers a statutory legal right to take over an enterprise when it is put up for sale, the subject of a takeover bid, or even facing closure or redundancies, would also spread ownership, wealth and power. Instead of capital hiring labour, labour hires capital and across Europe in regions like Emilia Romagna in Italy and Mondragon in Spain it has proved to be a successful and sustainable alternative to capitalism.

Beyond the state, the OECD has calculated that the UK pension market with £3 trillion in assets (2021) is the largest in Europe. And yet it is a slumbering giant. Pension and insurance funds could have a much bigger and more active role to play not least in direct primary investment.

The Strathclyde Local Government Pension Scheme alone is worth over £28 billion. At present it invests more in private equity unit trusts than any other type of investment market. Former and current public sector schemes make up most of the rest of the UK's highest valued with the Universities Superannuation Scheme the biggest. Electricity Supply, BT, Railways Pension Schemes are also in the top six: a reminder of the value of coordinating these reforms and actions on a UK-wide basis.

But in addition to this a Scottish Public Provident Fund bringing together 'funded' schemes and 'pay as you go' ones too, under one umbrella, could power change.

Whatever economic policy is developed it certainly requires something more radical than 'brand Scotland' when industries like energy, whisky, salmon are predominantly overseas owned.

It demands we look beyond the short-termism of the City of London and the under-resourcing of left behind communities due in part to the limitations of the Treasury's Green Book model.

We can renew and transition our economy to a net zero future, but we cannot make it just and equal while we continue to be, in effect, colonised by multinational corporations, global capital and financial markets.

To break from this economic model will require clear political leadership, but it will also need a movement inside the trade unions and in wider civic society, not only agitating and struggling for change but a movement that will keep that change going.

We must be prepared to take some risks, learn from international, as well as historical experience, to move from the old measures and structures, and to change horizons.

Our goal is to plant the seeds of a different future so that we have an economy which is of, by and for the people, and a political system whose democratic essence goes way beyond merely voting in elections.

This will require taking on vested interests, but if previous generations had not been prepared to overcome such challenges, much of what we value, would never have existed. With ambition, intelligence, courage and resolve, it can be done.

Building a Caring Economy

Sara Cowan

IN RECENT YEARS there's been growing recognition that the economy is not working for many people. Arguably, the economy has never really worked for most women. From the founding father of economic theory, Adam Smith, to more recent economic policy dominance of neoliberalism, there has been a critical omission in what is counted as having economic value. Care, for both people and planet, is excluded from what literally is counted in economic activity and in turn it is repeatedly omitted in economic policymaking. This omission is being increasingly recognised but action to tackle it is slow.

This chapter will make the case that economic policy needs to change at pace to tackle women's inequality and poverty, and a vital part of that change is seeing care as central to a successful economy. The chapter will briefly review recent evidence on women's economic position, before considering the role of care in determining women's position in the labour market and economy more widely. It finishes by outlining some of the steps required to begin to genuinely value care, and to deliver the economic and social equality that still eludes so many women 50 years after the publication of *The Red Paper on Scotland*.

As will be made clear in this chapter, understanding the experiences of women is central to making policy that tackles gender inequality. This was an omission in the original *Red Paper*. Of the 27 experts who wrote for *The Red Paper on Scotland* 50 years ago not one was a woman. This comment is not to diminish individuals' expertise but to highlight the missing voice and experience which is so often the case in economic debate and policy, despite many women being ready and able to make their case. This collection, edited by a woman and including women writers, will set a different tone in that regard. Building on these experiences is part of the process of tackling persistent inequality which has been at the heart of the *Red Paper* 'project'.

Long-term underinvestment in, and undervaluing of, care has been a hallmark of many economies and Scotland is no different, as the 2023 Oxfam report *A Scotland that cares...* makes clear. As most unpaid care is undertaken by women, its exclusion from economic value diminishes women's role in the paid labour market and impacts on all aspects of their lives. Women are more likely to be poor, have lower levels of savings and wealth, and are less able to increase paid work than men due to caring responsibilities. Overall, as the Close the Gap advocacy group illustrates in its 2018 briefing, women are more likely to be in lower-paid or insecure work, are twice as reliant on the social security system, and have lower and less access to pensions.

The Red Paper on Scotland investigated the economic challenges of the time. While these challenges and the context may have changed, some aspects are all too familiar. Society has moved on in many ways with regards to women and paid work, but much remains the same: women are still much more likely to take on unpaid care work and unpaid work within households, leading to different experiences for men and women of paid employment and unpaid work, and caring and provisioning for others. As *A Scotland that cares...* points out, around 70 per cent of unpaid care work is undertaken by women. My own organisation's research shows 80 per cent of those deemed 'inactive' in the labour market due to caring responsibilities are women. For many women, this means a greater reliance on public services and can limit the time they have for paid work and other activities.

Women and men continue to experience inequalities in pay, in employment and promotion opportunities, and in the harassment and abuse they experience at work. Analysis by the Scottish Trade Union Congress has found that the gender pay gap has recently risen by 30 per cent, from 6.4 per cent in 2023 to 8.3 per cent in 2024. This highlights that progress is not always linear and women have experienced setbacks especially through recent years of austerity, the Covid-19 pandemic and high inflation rates.

The UK Women's Budget Group (UK WBG) has found women are often the shock absorbers of poverty, tending to have the main responsibility for the purchase and preparation of food for their children and families and for the management of budgets in poor households. Taking on the stress of managing life in poverty.

This systemic inequality in our economy, as work undertaken in 2024 by the UK WBG has shown, means that recent austerity policies have hit particularly hard certain groups of women, with disabled women, women from minority ethnic backgrounds and single parents hit the hardest. The UK WBG found that between 2010 and 2024 women experienced a higher annual loss in living standards than men, losing 9.4 per cent (equivalent to £3,162 per year), to men's loss of 5.8 per cent (£2,395 per year). The poorest women faced a 21 per cent reduction in living standards, women from Black and Asian backgrounds a 13 per cent decline in living standards, and disabled women an 11 per cent decline in living standards. Glasgow Disability Alliance published research in March 2022 describing the 'triple whammy' that disabled women experienced during the pandemic, highlighting the 'combined and cumulative impact of being disabled, being a woman and dealing with Covid-19'.

Points in history such as the creation of the National Health Service have offered a step change, and we need a similar scale of vision with respect to care to make the transformative change women need. From the feminist economic perspective change is needed across economic policy to recognise the central role of care to our economy. Marilyn Waring, a New Zealand public scholar, parliamentarian (in the 1970s) and principal founder of feminist economics, demonstrated in her book *If Women Counted* how unpaid care and the value of nature were omitted from the system of national accounts which measures economic growth. This exclusion facilitates women's discrimination, contributing to the undervaluation of care. Recognising care work is therefore a vital step in building a gender-equal economy, and both economic policy and national and local budgets play a key role in achieving this.

Care work, both paid and unpaid, is overwhelmingly carried out by women and is a key sector in our economy. The current lack of investment in care must be recognised as both a cause and consequence of an unequal society. This undervaluation sustains stubborn poverty rates, entrenches gender inequality, leads to greater spending on emergency medical interventions and holds people back from living flourishing lives. According to 2022 Scottish Government figures, over a quarter of the people in receipt of social care support live in the most deprived areas, and unpaid carers in these areas are more likely to care for longer periods of time.

Yet, investing in care brings returns. In 2022 The Scottish Women's Budget Group (SWBG) modelled greater investment in adult social care and found that investing 3.7 per cent GDP in care, an increase of 1.8 per cent on the current budget, if used to widen access to care, improve carers' wages and increase carer numbers could create upwards of 75,000 jobs, both direct and indirect. With this come direct and indirect tax revenue that research estimated could yield £1.5 billion annually in 2022–3 prices, as well as spending in local economies. Analysis by UK WBG in 2020 found that investing 1 per cent GDP in care creates 2.7 times more jobs than the same investment in the construction industry. With women making up 83 per cent of the social care workforce, investing in care jobs is investing in women's jobs.

In turn, evidence from other countries demonstrates the role investment in childcare can bring to the economy. In Quebec a 2024 evaluation by Susan Prentice has shown returns of more the $3.50 for every $1 spent on childcare.

Economic policy and strategy have the capacity to tackle inequality or entrench it. Tweaks at the edges are not enough. Systemic change is required, as the prevailing neoliberal polices of the last 40 years have entrenched market-based solutions, which have only exacerbated long-standing problems in relation to care. Taking a feminist approach to the economy and budgetary processes starts by reflecting on the key values and outcomes for society and considering how to build an economic system that looks out for people and planet.

An essential part of the process of building an economy that values care and works for women is to build gender analysis into the decision-making process. Gender budget analysis is part of the feminist toolkit to build gender equality in Scotland. It seeks to bring the different economic realities of women and men to the heart of decision-making and, within this, recognising the differing experiences of women that intersect with the gender analysis, such as age, socio-economic status, disability, race, ethnicity, religion and rural or urban location. This process aims to shine a light on what experiences may be missing from the economic dialogue and try to rectify the understanding of this. To create lasting change for women there is a need to include this analysis in policy and budget decision-making at all levels of government.

Valuing care is not just a concept. There are specific actions required that can make a tangible difference to women's lives and more broadly tackle inequality. It starts with investment in care services, both childcare and adult social care, to build a system that puts wellbeing at the centre and invests in the people who are supported by it and the care workforce. Small steps have been taken in Scotland, but the pace of change is slow and not on the scale required to significantly tackle gender inequality. However, delivery of the real living wage in social care, and its promise in childcare, is progress. The next step will be for this care work to be recognised as skilled work and compensated on a scale that matches this skill. For social care, fixing this rate to a proportion of the average nurse's salary is one way of setting a relevant value. Research by SWBG in 2022 found that the rate at that time would be £15.20, compared to the real living wage at the time of £10.90.

However, current social care budgets do not meet people's needs, and this holds people back from achieving their potential and having their human rights upheld. It also transfers costs to acute services that people fall to at a faster rate when not supported at home. More investment is needed to increase access to care and quality of provision. This includes removing charges for care, which can be a barrier to access for those on the low incomes, with means-tested charging in Scotland starting for those with an income of £8,500 or more. Alongside greater investment it is critical that services are developed with the participation of those who use them, with local flexibility as part of a process of public sector renewal.

In childcare, provision of 1,140 hours funded hours to 3- and 4-year-olds is progress, however, challenges in accessing this offer demonstrate that, while it is an important start, it is not yet mission complete. Accessibility in its delivery needs to be improved as well as expansion to fall in line with the end of maternity pay. Targeting additional support to work for those on the lowest incomes first will work to tackle the multiple inequalities some women face.

Combined with investment in care is the need to provide time for both women and men to care. There is a need to redistribute caring and unpaid work responsibilities between women and men, and between the family and the state. This requires changes to parental leave policies to provide non-transferrable, equal entitlement to well-paid parental leave, as well as further development of carers-leave policies by both governments and business, to provide people with time to care without falling into poverty or needing to leave work. Changes to policy will support changing societal norms related to care. We know that care patterns for children are set in the first months of their lives, and the current provision of two weeks paternity leave does not cut it. In the long term, a four-day working week would be another step to providing time to care.

Ensuring people have access to a dignified safety net when they need it is another crucial element of making the economy work for women. Social security should provide everyone in society with a safety net and support when needed. Yet successive crises, including the Covid-19 pandemic and soaring inflation from 2021, highlight how inadequate the provisions are – and this hits women hardest as women have a greater reliance on social security. There are also areas where women will have particular needs, for example support to women who experience domestic abuse, or vulnerabilities that women face with no recourse to public funds. The challenge for Scotland is creating a caring social security system and, using the powers available in Scotland, to increase incomes and lift people out of poverty. Greater levers are held at Westminster to transform the system and scale of the safety net, and it is at this level we need to see substantial change. An urgent increase in the value of social security benefits is needed to provide a guarantee that people can meet life's essentials, as well as ending harmful policies, such as the benefits cap and the two-child limit and the blanket use of 'no recourse to public funds'. In the long term, options such as a Minimum Income Guarantee could be put in place to provide the necessary safety net as part of a more comprehensive approach linking income and access to services.

How these changes are paid for has a role to play in tackling inequality too. Decisions about how best to raise public funds through tax can affect women and men differently. In Scotland, as across the UK, the unequal taxation of income from wealth and income from work represents a tax break for wealthy men. We need to see government decisions at all levels that build fairness into our tax system, and that work together with public spending decisions to tackle inequality. This requires a wealth tax as part of the basket of tax options.

With concerted effort an economy that works for women and men is possible. Recognising, valuing and investing in care is a critical element to deliver the changes that women need to see and redressing the balance in the current economic system. A gender-equal economy will be one that works better for everybody, especially those who currently face the sharp end of economic inequality. It will be an economy that respects and protects nature, taking action head-on to respond to climate change and tackle inequality. It will be an economy that cares for people and planet.

Scottish Trade Unions:
A Force for Change

Introduction

Frieda Park

THAT OUR WORLD has changed in 50 years is no surprise, nor should we be surprised that it has changed in ways that were unforeseen by the then activists in the labour movement. But what has been most difficult to reckon with is just how negative much of that change has been, representing a turning of the tide against organised labour and the left. This section of the *Red Paper* looks at why these changes happened and how trade unions have responded to the continued necessity to represent their members' interests and defend the working class. This includes taking on broader structural changes and the nature of the world which we live in with war, increasing arms spending and confrontation diverting much-needed resources from productive and social spending.

In 1975, despite the inevitable ebb and flow of successes and setbacks in the struggles of workers domestically and internationally, the overall arc still seemed to be one of progress and possibilities for a better life for all. The strength of the labour movement was demonstrated in the wave of industrial action in the '70s, including the Upper Clyde Shipbuilders' work-in of 1971, and the passing of the *Equal Pay Act 1970* and the *Sex Discrimination Act 1975* greatly enhancing women's rights at work. Yet looking back the time could also be seen to be the highpoint of these expectations and on the brink of a watershed, with the election of the Tories led by Margaret Thatcher only four years later. The era of neoliberalism that Thatcher ushered in ultimately put an end to the expectations of working-class people that their children's lives would be better than their own, that there would be continuously rising living standards and that the welfare state would be relied on to support us from the cradle to the grave.

Also in the '70s, the world was moving from a period of Cold War to one of détente between the Soviet Union and the United States. The trade union movement along with the peace movement played an important role in pressing for peace and disarmament. Now we face a world which has been made unstable by the United States' unbridled ambition to maintain its hegemony, and wars and the threat of war are everywhere.

The economic, political and social changes which happened from the '80s until the present day were not just plans hatched by Margaret Thatcher, nor even of British capital alone, but were part of a worldwide transformation of globalisation and 'free' markets dominated by the wealthiest countries. In Scotland, as elsewhere, that meant de-industrialisation and the privatisation of industries and services. The consequences of this ran deep. Along with the industries and jobs, so also declined trade union membership. The impact of these losses was not just a numbers game but had a highly corrosive effect on communities, collective identity and the means of engaging in progressive and socialist politics. Hope for the future was squashed, leaving people demoralised. No wonder that other alternatives won support – the belief that independence for Scotland, unanchored to class struggle, would provide change.

Since Labour won the 2024 election there have been some positive moves like settling the public sector pay disputes and the repeal of some Tory anti-union legislation, but also disastrous ones like depriving the majority of pensioners of their Winter Fuel Allowance, denying compensation to the WASPI (Women Against State Pension Inequality) women and retaining the two-child benefit cap. Trade unions are at the forefront of opposing austerity-style policies and demanding more from Labour, including trying to maximise the benefits to workers of the New Deal for working people. This demonstrates that, despite the challenges facing the movement, trade unions remain the most important vehicle for working-class action, political influence and solidarity.

The authors in this section look at diverse aspects of the trade unions and working-class politics, how the decades of neoliberalism have impacted on particular areas, and positive developments in the movement to respond to the circumstances we are now in.

In his chapter 'Trade Unionism and Class Power: From Control to Voice', Diarmaid Kelliher examines the shift over the last 50 years from advocacy for workers' control and industrial democracy, which were widely debated in the '70s, to what now appears to be tokenism at best. The radicalism of worker buy-outs and control, or of workers having equal say on the boards of companies, has been replaced by weaker commitments on an 'employee voice' as set out in Scotland by the SNP Government's Fair Work Convention. Neoliberalism promoted individualism over collectivism, undermining working-class cohesion and identity, and set out to crush the unions through legislation and the power of the state – as used against the miners in their historic strike of 1984–5. The conclusion is that power is critical and that only when the labour movement is strong will its voice be meaningful. A powerful movement is necessary to lead to change both in the political and the industrial spheres.

As a long serving officer in the Public and Commercial Services Union (PCS), Lynn Henderson is well placed to examine the changing devolution settlement and its impact on workers in the civil service in Scotland. In her chapter 'Public and Civil Service Transformed by Trade Unionists', she looks at the changing nature of what a civil service job means, especially for women workers who make up 54 per cent of the civil service workforce, and 65 per cent of PCS membership. She explores the impact on civil servants of the transfer of their employment from UK government departments to working directly for Scottish agencies. She describes how PCS has actively engaged with its members over their priorities and is clear about its role in representing their interests, whatever the constitutional settlement.

A grassroots campaigning perspective is provided by Arthur West and Tommy Morrison who are long-term Trades Union Council (TUC) activists. In their chapter they describe the unique role of local TUCs in bringing together local trade union bodies and communities to campaign on issues affecting their members and localities. The article describes TUC's work specifically on promoting peace and disarmament and opposition to the Trident nuclear weapons system. This is a vital bread and butter issue for trade unionists as money spent on warfare and armaments is money not spent on welfare and jobs.

These diverse articles are united by common themes. That the effective power of the unions is in their democratic structures and membership, as the recent wave of industrial action demonstrated. That neither constitutional change nor changes of government on their own will deliver for the working class without trade union members taking action and making demands in the political sphere. Trade Unions are a powerful democratic force representing the interests of workers and their communities and are at the forefront of pressing for progressive policies: on equalities and representation; on democratic accountability; on solidarity; and for a peaceful world in which we can again look forward to children's futures being better than their parents.

Trade Unionism and Class Power: From Control to Voice

Diarmaid Kelliher

IN HIS INTRODUCTION to *The Red Paper on Scotland* 1975, Gordon Brown described a

> surging forward of demands by trade unionists for real control over the decisions affecting their livelihoods.

The book included a chapter on 'Industrial Democracy and Workers Control' written by Alex Ferry, a leading engineering trade unionist. Ferry's thinking reflected a long-standing tendency in the labour movement to equate industrial democracy with free collective bargaining, but also attempts in the 1960s and 1970s to promote a more substantive form of economic control from below. Fifty years later, little appears to remain of the workers' control agenda. Instead, the terminology of 'employee voice' has become popular in certain political circles. Tracing the development of this debate from the original *Red Paper* to the present day tells us much about the trajectories of trade unionism, economic democracy, and class power relations in Scotland and Britain.

The Red Paper's front cover features an image of the 1971 UCS work-in, an event that was emblematic of contemporary attempts by workers to assert control in the face of industrial restructuring. Occupations or work-ins were one expression of this mood, intimately connected to social audits and alternative corporate plans, developed most famously at Lucas Aerospace. In addition, there was a spate of new worker co-operatives, including the short-lived *Scottish Daily News*. The Institute for Workers' Control, founded in 1968, attempted to coalesce these somewhat sporadic events into a broader movement. Such experiments weren't entirely novel, of course. Nevertheless, their flourishing reflected growing dissatisfaction with the hierarchical bureaucracies of the post-war economy, in both the public and private sectors, and the increasing problems facing British industry.

In 1973, Harold Wilson suggested that

the pressure for a greater degree of workers' democracy in whatever form [...] is only in its infancy. There is little doubt that we are at the beginning of a social revolution in this sphere.

Two years later, the Labour Government announced an enquiry into industrial democracy. The resulting 'Bullock Report' (1977) recommended requiring that the boards of large firms have equal representation of shareholders and employees, with an additional smaller group of co-opted directors. Transport and General Workers' Union (TGWU) General Secretary Jack Jones was a prominent advocate of this measure. He believed that unions were influential at the scales of the workplace and national economic planning, but not in between, at the level of company policy and strategy.

The influence of 1970s trade unions at all these scales can be overestimated. Nevertheless, in certain sectors, strong union organisation created a counterweight to management power in the workplace. A form of direct control was also asserted through industrial action. The Bullock debate took place in the aftermath of the early 1970s strike wave, the most significant industrial unrest since 1926, which saw several prominent successes. It was also true that trade unions had some role in high-level economic discussions, for example through the National Economic Development Council, established in 1962.

The Bullock recommendations, however, were abandoned. Business lobbying and hostility from certain cabinet *members* helped scotch the idea, as did scepticism from some unions. There was a view within sections of the labour movement that worker participation was class collaborationism; others were apparently opposed because they felt that the plans risked diminishing trade union officials in favour of local shop stewards. One Scottish survey found that workplace representatives themselves were divided over the issue, although clearly more amenable than management. The highly visible debates on economic democracy in the 1970s show that employers' 'right to manage' was being openly contested. But the failure of both Bullock and the grassroots movement for economic democracy emphasised the significant limits of workers' power in this decade. The situation, of course, was about to get worse.

The Conservatives' 1979 election victory banished industrial democracy from the Government's agenda. Thatcherism did, however, have its own ideas about popular empowerment. The right had long viewed individual property ownership as the antidote to labour movement demands for collective control. Under Thatcher, state-subsidised privatisation of council housing was the most obvious expression of this. But measures to widen share ownership can also be understood as an attempt to create a 'popular capitalism'. Privatisations in the 1980s were often accompanied by employee ownership schemes. BT was a notable example, with over 95 per cent of its eligible workers taking shares. But, crucially, employees still owned less than 5 per cent of the new company. Some elements of the right also showed an interest in co-operatives. The infamous 1977 'Ridley Report' recommended that the best way to deal with the National Coal Board was to 'break [it] down into pits, and seek to form worker co-operatives wherever possible'. John Redwood's support for the Tower Colliery workers' buyout in 1995 can be understood in this context.

There was, however, no great flourishing of co-operatives or employee ownership, much less control. The Conservatives demonstrated greater vigour in their attacks on trade unions than in their attempts to create alternative forms of popular economic participation. The notion of company-level trade union representation could be ignored, and tripartite arrangements sidelined, but defeating workplace-level trade unionism required a more active strategy. The Conservatives shifted focus from the democratic deficit of the workplace to that of the trade unions themselves. New laws mandating union elections and secret strike ballots were introduced alongside other measures that chipped away at the power of the labour movement. Those who resisted – most famously the miners – faced the full force of the British state. The defeat of the 1984–5 strike sent a signal to the wider movement about their diminished role in society.

There had been a brief flourishing of Joint Consultative Committees in the 1970s. These were mostly abandoned by employers in the 1980s as the political context shifted dramatically. Trade union density and collective bargaining coverage declined precipitously, nearly halving in each case over the period of Thatcher's and Major's governments. The experience of the 1980s significantly undermined the participative nature of trade unionism, however partial this may have been, in favour of a 'servicing' model and the 'new realism' of partnership with employers. This wasn't, however, partnership in the sense of co-determination or worker participation; it was an extremely misaligned relationship.

Broader economic patterns – globalisation, financialisation, deindustrialisation, neoliberalism – clearly played an important role in undercutting workers' power. These were transnational processes, of course, the causes of which far exceeded Thatcherism. Nevertheless, government policy in Britain facilitated these trends. The acceleration of deindustrialisation in 1980s Britain proved particularly difficult for the labour movement to deal with, as it tended to undercut sectors with existing trade union strength. Scottish workers' distance from economic power grew in multiple ways. Corporate ownership became concentrated in southern England, with headquarters and research and development increasingly based in London.

The Labour Party also went through a process of embracing neoliberalism, otherwise known as 'modernisation'. The 1997 manifesto promised that there would be 'no return' to the industrial relations of the 1970s, but instead the 'basic minimum rights of the individual' at work would be enhanced, and there would be greater partnership between employers and employees. This was an explicit rejection of collectivism. There were some gestures towards bolstering trade union presence and employee input in the workplace through the introduction of statutory recognition procedures and the 2004 Information and Consultation of Employees (ICE) Regulations. But it was thin gruel. The ICE regulations, the result of a European directive, required only very limited workplace consultation. Statutory recognition didn't halt the slide in collective bargaining. This was particularly the case in the private sector where, by one measure, coverage fell from 22 to 16.8 per cent of workplaces across the period of New Labour. Unions may not have been the avowed enemy that they were in the 1980s, but nor were workers in control.

New Labour's collapse was marked by the economic and political tumult of the 2007–8 crash, followed by the brutal austerity of the Conservative–Liberal Democrat coalition, and the two referendums on Scottish independence and UK withdrawal from the EU. These upheavals appeared to remind some mainstream politicians in the 2010s of the existence of social class, even if it was frequently constructed in reactionary terms. The 'take back control' narrative in some ways also lent itself to re-engaging with economic democracy. Just a few months after becoming Prime Minister in 2016, Theresa May told the Conservative Party Conference of her plan

> to have not just consumers represented on company boards, but workers as well. Because we are the party of workers.

May soon recalled that the Conservatives were not, after all, the party of workers, and backtracked in a speech to the CBI. What remained was a revision of the British Corporate Governance Code that encouraged listed companies to involve employees with representation on boards as one means of doing so. Very few chose that route, and even for those that did – workers' champion Sports Direct for example – it was usually tokenistic.

In 2013, the TUC began to call for worker representation on boards as a key mechanism for the enhancement of 'workers' voice'. By 2019, Labour was essentially following the TUC's lead in its manifesto pledge that elected worker-directors would fill one-third of company boards. Under Jeremy Corbyn's leadership, the party demonstrated its greatest interest since the Bullock era in questions of workers' participation, ownership and control. Serious consideration was given to expanding multiple forms of public ownership in ways that avoided the democratic limitations of the post-1945 nationalisations. Labour also developed plans for Inclusive Ownership Funds, in which 10 per cent of shares of large companies would be owned and managed collectively by their workers, increasing not just the share of wealth held by employees but also their influence over decisions. 'Workers' voice' was again an important rationale for the policy.

According to Wes Streeting, writing in a Fabian Society Tract in 2020, the inclusive ownership funds were 'the most outrageous policy' in the 2019 manifesto. Neither they, nor workers on boards, survived the change of Labour leadership in 2020. At the time of writing, Labour's *New Deal for Working People*, which outlines its plans for employment policy, insists awkwardly that the party 'will back working people to take their voice back'. There is a section on 'voice at work' but the actual plans could generously be described as modest. The proposed electronic balloting would be welcome, undoubtedly, as would the simplification of the statutory recognition process and the extension of sectoral bargaining to adult social care. But overall, there has been a retreat from anything resembling economic democracy into tweaking at the edges of collective bargaining.

Similar trends are evident in Holyrood politics as well. 'Employee voice' is one of the Scottish Government's National Performance Indicators and is measured by collective bargaining coverage. The Fair Work Convention, an independent advisory body to Scottish Ministers, offers a somewhat more expansive definition of 'effective voice', which

> can include approaches to trade union recognition and collective bargaining; direct and indirect involvement and participation; communication and consultation arrangements and procedures that give scope to individuals and groups to air their views, be listened to and influence outcomes.

Although the evidence on collective bargaining coverage isn't always reliable, there is good reason to believe that a higher proportion of Scottish workers are covered than any other part of the UK. Scotland also has a distinct pattern of national and industry-level agreements. Public sector employees – who constitute more than a fifth of Scottish workers – are far more likely to be covered than private ones. Due to the composition of the sector, this means more women and older workers have their conditions formally negotiated by unions.

Nevertheless, there is a broad convergence of Westminster and Holyrood politics around the importance of employee 'voice' – taken more or less seriously – with a simultaneous absence of anything substantially resembling economic democracy, never mind workers' control. The shift from control, or even participation, to voice in part represents merely a fashion for particular terminology. But it also marks the significant diminishment of the labour movement since the days of the first *Red Paper on Scotland*. 'Voice' risks being synonymous with the kind of insubstantial consultation that characterises much contemporary policy implementation.

The question of power is crucial here; it is only when the labour movement is strong that its voice becomes meaningful. There is no simple solution, of course. But the answer won't be found exclusively in either union organising or at the level of state policy. The workplace and the political sphere must be simultaneous sites of struggle if Scottish workers are to gain 'real control over the decisions affecting their livelihoods'.

Public and Civil Service:
Transformed by Trade Unionists

Lynn Henderson

THE ORGANISED WORKFORCE in civil and public services has fundamentally changed in the 50 years since Gordon Brown edited the first *Red Paper on Scotland*. Back then joining the civil service was seen as a good opportunity for young school leavers, in the era before working-class access to university became widespread. My older sister left school at 16 and joined the Department of Health and Social Care (DHSS) in Edinburgh, with my family believing she was made for life. In the new towns of East Kilbride and Cumbernauld, many local people automatically went from school to the Inland Revenue, where they stayed until retirement.

For women workers however, there was an additional consideration. Although the civil service marriage bar was abolished in 1946 for Home Civil Servants, it was retained until 1973 for the Foreign Service. Until then, women were required to resign from their civil service post upon marriage. This changed when the *Sex Discrimination Act 1975* required women in the civil service to be treated the same as men.

While around 54 per cent of all civil servants are now women, they make up 65 per cent of members of the Public and Commercial Services Union (PCS), the trade union recognised across all grades in the civil service structure. On the retirement of PCS General Secretary, Mark Serwotka, in January 2024 after 23 years in the role, PCS elected its first woman General Secretary, Fran Heathcote – who is playing a very active role across the labour and trade union movement, particularly in her high-profile solidarity with the people of Palestine.

Over the last 25 years, our devolved Scottish governance has developed, actively operating tax-varying powers and administering social security more recently, moving substantially beyond the territory referenced in the 1975 'Devolution and Democracy' chapter by David Gow. Back then, most significance was dedicated to questions around oil prices, the centrality of the Scottish Development Agency exercising economic powers, and, interestingly, the strength of powers of Labour, the Communist Party and

Trotskyist control over unions.

Now, as the war in the Middle East expands, we are currently in danger of returning to an oil crisis similar to that of the 1970s. Economic powers remains a live debate in Scotland. The strength of the Labour Party in Scotland took a massive downward plunge over the last decade, with the rise of the SNP. The 2024 UK election result saw substantial regains for Labour as the SNP in power has somewhat lost political trust of many. The Communist Party and Trotskyist forces in the trade union movement remain present, if marginal.

In *The Red Paper on Scotland 2005*, Professor Gregor Gall analysed union density in Scotland generally, concluding that relative to England, it is higher, but less so than in Wales or Northern Ireland, and no more than in parts of England such as the Midlands. Whilst the truth around the decline of union premium is now generally accepted across academic circles, there remains some romantic political rhetoric within the movement that somehow, Scots remain more likely to join a trade union. In the civil service, many young members are now recruited into graduate fast track programmes, and unions like PCS work hard to reach out and encourage them to join and actively participate in their trade union. Often these new workers regard unions as something perhaps their grandparents were members of, as many of their parents' generation's working life has been marred by industrial decline, public sector cuts and privatisation – resulting in insecure work, lower pay, and poorer terms and conditions.

I wrote a chapter entitled 'Yes, Minister, in the thick of it' for *Class, Nation and Socialism: The Red Paper on Scotland 2014*. It discussed the potential role of a distinct and separate Scottish Civil Service on the eve of the Referendum on Independence held on 18 September that year. I concluded that a class focus for organised public sector workers remained more important than either unionist or nationalist visions of government.

At that time, my union, PCS, undertook a widespread dialogue with our Scottish members across the civil service and related areas – in both UK reserved and Scottish devolved departments, agencies and non-departmental public bodies (NDPBs). We were keen to ascertain what kind of Scotland they wished to live in. The response was, in the main, that PCS members were specifically interested in how pay, pensions, terms and conditions and job security would be impacted in transitioning a UK Crown Civil Service to that of an Independent Scotland. Perhaps it should be no surprise that workers facing such a transition, are likely to respond to their union about their immediate industrial interests, rather than on wider socio-economic, cultural or democratic matters.

As I write, a decade after the rejection of independence in the 2014 referendum, and in the post-Corbyn era of Labour leadership, we are approaching the first 100 days and the first Budget of a mainstream Labour Westminster Government led by Sir Keir Starmer. Declining support at the polls between July and October 2024 reflect revelations of Starmer, his family and key Ministers taking thousands of pounds of clothes and gifts, while maintaining the two-child benefit cap and ending the Winter Fuel Allowance for a majority of pensioners.

We are also witnessing SNP decline after a generation of holding power in Scotland. Legislation on the New Deal for Working People, restoring trade union rights, and some concessions on inflation-proofed public sector pay were dangled ahead of the autumn TUC annual Congress and the Labour Party Conference.

PCS as a union in Scotland has significantly changed over the last decade too. In 2014, only a third of the 30,000 PCS members in Scotland worked within the devolved Scottish Government sector. The majority of civil servants in Scotland, post-devolution, were retained in UK-wide departments with offices in different parts of Scotland. By far the largest number of civil servants worked in the Department for Work and Pensions (DWP), His Majesty's Revenue and Customs (HMRC) and the Home Office (passport, immigration, customs and border force services), among others.

With increasing devolution of tax powers and social security specifically, there has been an increase in Scottish devolved services and workforce, including the creation of new bodies such as the Scottish Social Security Agency and Revenue Scotland. This expansion of devolved government jobs in Scotland has occurred alongside a net decline in UK civil service jobs in Scotland, and elsewhere, under successive Tory governments. The resultant effect has been that the majority of the PCS membership in Scotland are now employed in the Scottish devolved sector, rather than in the UK reserved departments and agencies. This in turn impacts on how our union operates in Scotland.

Whilst pay is devolved to the Scottish Public Sector Pay Remit for those civil servants employed by Scottish Government departments, agencies and NDPBs, the status of the workforce – whether in devolved or reserved areas – remains fixed as servants of the Crown, subject to the so-called impartiality restrictions determined by the Civil Service Code. In the fag-end days of the Sunak Government, right-wing Tory Ministers sought to rein in civil servants in some departments from wearing Pride rainbow lanyards or undertaking charitable collections money for the Medical Aid for Palestinians, suggesting that these might be in breach of the Civil Service Code.

Although there has been no transition to a wholly Scottish Civil Service, nor any real demand for it from the workforce, there have been significant developments in PCS Union structures and internal democracy in Scotland (and Wales) since 2014, that I believe are for the better.

Margaret Thatcher abolished central collective bargaining on pay in the 1980s. This led to pay inequality and disharmony across government departments that has now reached crisis point. Following devolution, the Scottish Government implemented a centralised Scottish Government Public Sector Pay Remit, with delegated negotiations taking place with the unions in each employer bargaining unit – effectively Thatcher's policy with a kilt on. This has been to the relative advantage of PCS members working under a more progressive devolved government than their UK equivalents. There has been no compulsory redundancy guarantee in place since 2009, a commitment to the Scottish Living Wage, Fair Work agreements, relatively better percentage pay increases and a growing commitment to the reduced working week. However, as devolved government operates within the Barnett formula set by the UK Government, many of these advantages have been marginal. Our union has often referred to the pay remit under both Labour and SNP administrations as merely passing down the UK remit with a 'tartan cover'.

There is a growing industrial cohesion across PCS Scottish Government sector bargaining units, and an increasing demand for the journey towards Pay Coherence to escalate. This will be particularly pertinent now that there is a Labour Government at UK level, and the SNP Scottish Government will be keen to continue being just one foot to the left of Labour. A restructuring of our lay Scottish Sector Forum is underway to ensure that there is wider leverage of members from across the sector at all stages of negotiation with Scottish Ministers.

Beyond employer bargaining, our union has expanded its democratic base in Scotland and in 2023 held direct elections for all members in Scotland to a new Scottish Nation Executive. At the same time, a founding conference was held in Autumn 2023 to establish an annual Scottish Policy Conference. This is a massive democratic breakthrough with policy making on devolved issues being debated and decided in Scotland and implemented by an executive directly accountable to the membership. The class inequalities, poverty and exclusion in Scottish societies impacts workers across sectors, and within the government sector, across UK and devolved employers. For the first time, PCS members in Scotland regardless of employer, will be able to determine the union's position on those key socio-economic issues that impact on all our members as citizens of Scotland.

While the debate in Scotland remains fixed on increased devolution versus independence, the workforce responsible for government services remains firmly unionised, and actively participating in their collective industrial interest.

Scottish Trade Unions:
Fighting for Peace and Justice

Thomas Morrison & Arthur West

THIS CHAPTER WILL look at the efforts of trade union bodies, particularly locally based Trades Union Councils, to contribute to building a peaceful world through dialogue and diplomacy between countries rather than recourse to war.

Trade Union organisations involved in the struggle for peace are faced with a world where political violence and war have become an everyday reality in too many parts of our planet. The US-led invasions of Afghanistan (2001) and Iraq (2003) marked the start of an escalating era of wars including in Libya, Syria, Yemen and Nagorno-Karabakh. Currently there are wars burning in Gaza, Lebanon, Sudan and Ukraine, with peace-making efforts being sidelined.

At the time of writing most media outlets agree that over 40,000 Palestinians have been killed in Israel's current war on Gaza. Many thousands of people have been killed or injured as a result of the Russia–Ukraine war which has been ongoing since February 2022.

The Campaign for Nuclear Disarmament (CND) reports that Starmer's Labour Government seems equally as keen as the previous Tory administration to renew the Trident nuclear weapons system. Current estimates suggest that this will cost the eye-watering sum of £205 billion. As CND rightly says, this money could be better spent on jobs, homes, and improving the lives of the British people without threatening the lives of others.

Given threats to peace and the war-mongering attitudes prevalent in today's world, trade union-based campaigning for a more peaceful world is fraught with difficulties. Even in such difficult times we can recognise and build upon the positive interactions between the Scottish peace movement and trade union bodies such as Trades Union Councils.

Rank and file activists in trade unions in Scotland work through their trade unions but can also use a different route to influence the Scottish Trade Union Congress (STUC) – that of Trades Union Councils. These are local groups of trade unionists elected from trade union branches whose members live and/or work in the area. This gives them a more community-based focus and means they can work across different trade unions and with local activists.

Trades Union Councils can play a more prominent role in the Scottish labour movement compared to the rest of Britain as they have a direct input into the STUC Congress, with the right to move and to amend motions on the preliminary agenda and the same right to speak as representatives from affiliated trade unions. A review of STUC agendas shows that the more progressive motions come from the rank and file of the movement, the Trades Union Councils.

A number of Trades Union Council motions have called for a more peaceful world and to utilise the skills of defence workers in other areas of the economy. Due mainly to these motions the STUC has had a long-standing position of opposition to the Trident nuclear weapons system. There is, however, scepticism from GMB and parts of Unite the Union about whether the Scottish economy can diversify and be less reliant on the defence sector.

In the mid-1990s Clydebank TUC submitted a motion on Trident to an STUC Congress. Workers from Faslane protested outside the conference hall with placards calling for the motion to be opposed. Yet the arguments contained in the motion and made clear from the rostrum always took on board the concerns of the workers and their unions while condemning these weapons of mass destruction. Fortunately, as the years passed this once-controversial motion from Clydebank TUC was built on, as Trades Union Council motions in support of a Scottish Defence Diversification Agency were passed by convincing majorities.

The STUC and Scottish trade unionists have a long tradition of campaigning in support of workers in struggle in other countries. During the time of the original *Red Paper on Scotland,* workers at Rolls Royce were boycotting work on aircraft engines for the Pinochet dictatorship in Chile. Throughout the 1980s the STUC joined anti-apartheid campaigners demanding sanctions against South Africa. It has continued to support the people of Cuba through their campaigns for the release of the Miami Five and against the inhumane sanctions imposed by the us. The STUC has long campaigned against Israel's treatment of Palestinians and campaigned for a two-state solution. In recent years Trades Councils and some trade unions have put forward motions highlighting the abuse of workers in Qatar during World Cup preparations, and the treatment of women in Afghanistan.

At the 2023 STUC Congress several motions were submitted by Trades Union Councils on the war in Ukraine. For example, the motion from

Aberdeen TUC argued for a cessation of hostilities in Ukraine and a settlement that fully protected and embedded the rights of both Ukrainian and Russian-speaking communities. A motion from Clydebank TUC made the point that the trade union movement should stand in solidarity with ordinary Ukrainians and demand an immediate withdrawal of Russian troops. The motion also condemned any attempts by NATO to escalate the conflict. It added that NATO was not a progressive force for peace in the world and that its expansion into Eastern Europe in the 1990s and 2000s had not been a helpful development. These were incorporated into a composite motion which was replaced by a General Council statement which stated, 'The General Council reiterates its opposition to direct NATO intervention in the war'.

At the 2024 STUC Congress delegates backed calls for an end to the recently announced ramping up of arms spending by almost 20 per cent in just three years. This position came about because Congress supported motions submitted by Clydebank, Glasgow, Midlothian, North Lanarkshire, East Ayrshire and North Ayrshire Trades Union Councils. Following debate on the motions a General Council statement was passed which committed Congress to being an 'educator for, and a campaigner on peace'. The statement also called for investment in re-skilling arms industry workers to support other challenges such as meeting targets to transition away from carbon-heavy industries.

At the same Congress delegates condemned Israel's invasion of Gaza as well as the failure of most political parties to call for a halting of weapons sales to Israel. In an emotional session Congress adopted a General Council statement on the war on Gaza. Prior to the statement delegates watched video contributions, first from Masa Hlelel, a volunteer firefighter from Nablus, who made it clear that Palestinians were aware that thousands of people across Scotland and the world were in support of peace and justice for the Palestinian people. This was followed by a contribution from the Palestinian Federation of Trade Unions representative, Shaher Sa'ed, who declared, 'This is our land and we are not going anywhere'. Finally, Palestine's Ambassador to the UK, Husam Zomlot, spoke, condemning Israel for imposing famine on over two million Palestinian people. Mr Zomlot also mentioned that in the West Bank hundreds had been killed in settler violence and thousands of people had been detained without charge. Following these contributions and discussion of a range of motions mainly put forward by Trades Union Councils, Congress agreed a General Council statement which affirmed targeted support for the Boycott, Divestment and Sanctions campaign and an end to arms sales to Israel.

The 2024 Congress discussions on military spending and Palestine demonstrate that Trades Union Councils can play an influential and important role in promoting progressive policies within the trade union movement. Ensuring that progressive policy statements and motions are supported at STUC Congress and other trade union forums is not enough, however; there is also a need to spread awareness around peace and disarmament issues at grassroots level within the Scottish trade union movement.

In Scotland, as the home of the Trident submarine base, the issue of nuclear disarmament has been of particular importance. One response was to establish the Scottish Trade Union Peace Network at the end of 2022. Presently this network involves Trades Union Council representatives, but it is open to participation from trade union representatives and individual members. The Network disseminates information across the Scottish trade union movement on the need for diplomacy and negotiation rather than war to resolve tensions between countries and regions of the world. It produces a regular bulletin giving information on peace movement events, the threat of nuclear weapons, and how military spending can divert funds away from important public services such as health and education. One of its campaigning points is that Trident sustains only a small number of jobs (around 7,000) compared to its cost. Investment alternatives such as renewable energy projects would generate more jobs at appropriate skill levels. A major programme of offshore wind and wave power, for example, could create 25–30,000 new jobs. It is dangerous for communities to be dependent on one employer or industry. Diversification is both possible and essential and would safeguard workers' futures.

The Peace Network is promoting three key messages. Firstly, Trident replacement would come at a massive cost. Scottish CND research suggests that this figure could be around £205 billion. This money could be better spent in areas such as education, health and dealing with the scourge of child poverty. Secondly, there is a very high cost for each job in Trident related work. As the Reid Foundation has stated expenditure on Trident offers little to the Scottish and UK economies by way of economic activity and the money spent does not have a multiplier effect. And finally, in recent times Scotland has seen a massive loss of jobs in local government and frontline workers can testify to chronic staff shortages in areas such as health and social care. As the Reid Foundation has also stated, even a modest transfer of funds from Trident spending could stem the loss of jobs and staff shortages in these vital lifeline services.

Back in 2007 the Scottish Trade Union Congress and Scottish CND published a study entitled *Cancelling Trident* which examined the economic and employment consequences for Scotland. The report did a very good job of exposing the exaggerated claims of job losses among defence workers in the event of scrapping the Trident programme. In 2015 another report produced by the STUC and Scottish CND provided a timely addition to the previous study. This second report highlighted how the austerity policies of the Tory-led Government of 2010–15 had squeezed defence budgets. The report clearly demonstrated that pursuing Trident replacement was at the expense of spending on conventional defence and other areas of public spending such as health and education. It included two important case studies from the United States which made a compelling case that, with early planning and workforce involvement, communities can do very well economically and socially after the closure of military installations.

The two STUC-SCND reports were followed in 2016 by a report from the respected Reid Foundation called *Trident and its Successor Programme*. This report provided a summary of the case for non-renewal of Trident and employment diversification. There is therefore a body of work in these reports which outlines the moral and economic case for an end to UK nuclear weapons.

In 1968 the UK signed the Nuclear Non-Proliferation Treaty which was supposed to commit the country to nuclear disarmament. However now more than 50 years later, we are developing a replacement for the current Trident nuclear weapons system. It now seems to be the time for the trade union movement to redouble its efforts to get rid of nuclear weapons and free up some of the vast sums of money for decent things like health and education and dealing with the damage which climate change is causing the planet.

The need for a well-supported and diverse peace movement working in partnership with trade union structures is more vital than ever.

Where We Are and Where Next

Introduction

Coll McCail

THE SHOUT OF the welder. *The Speak of the Mearns*. The discourse of the Enlightenment. These 'echoes from the past', hoped Donald Dewar in July 1999, would guide the new Scottish Parliament and direct the work of its members as they sought to shape Scotland for the new millennium. A quarter of a century ago, this promise of a 'people's parliament' granted fresh impetus to those struggling for Scotland's political and economic democratisation – and hope that, for Scotland's young people, things would be different.

There was genuine belief that the rich tapestry of movements that convened to campaign for an end to the democratic deficit might see their ambitions reflected first on the Royal Mile and, five years later, at Holyrood – where Alasdair Gray's words were concretised on the Canongate Wall and Mick McGahey's ashes were scattered in the foundations of the debating chamber.

Two months after Donald Dewar's speech, Jimmy Reid issued a more cautious warning in the pages of *The Guardian*. 'We don't want a gravy train for the well-connected few,' wrote the leader of Upper Clyde Shipbuilders work-in as he raged against the myopia which plagued Parliament's early days. Regrettably, Reid's warning was quickly forgotten as the domestic political class to which the new Parliament gave birth grew ever more comfortable. Devolution, viewed less as an evolving process than a static constitutional arrangement, gradually ground to a halt. As the process of devolving power stalled, so too did the prospect of transforming the fortunes of the nation's young people.

Today, Donald Dewar's hopes for the Scottish Parliament have been scrambled. The shout of the welder has been muffled by a bipartisan neoliberal agenda that courts foreign direct investment but disregards domestic industrial strategy. The failure to save the Grangemouth oil refinery in late 2024 – and the more than 2,000 jobs that depend on it – is, as Rosie Hampton explains, only the latest example of this capitulation to corporate interests.

The speak of the Mearns has been silenced by Holyrood's chronic failure to tackle Scotland's archaic patterns of land ownership – just over 400 individuals own 50 per cent of private land in rural Scotland. Rather than hold these lords and lairds accountable, Holyrood opts to perpetually entrench their power and influence. In 2022, for example, the largest recipients of the Scottish Government's Farm Payments were the Duke of Buccleuch (£3.5 million), the Earl of Moray (£1.7 million) and the Duke of Roxburghe (£1.4 million).

The discourse of the Enlightenment, meanwhile, is insulted by its contemporary inheritors. Far from working as if they live in the early days of a better nation, the 'nest of fearties' presently installed in the Scottish Parliament prefer punitive and performative prohibitions – be they on plastic bags, alcohol-branded pint glasses, drinking booze on trains or smoking electronic vapes – to systemic action aimed at tackling the root of Scotland's deeply ingrained, structurally determined social problems. As Gavin Brewis notes, such attitudes have dogged devolution's 25-year history, from Jack McConnell's 'War on NEDs' right up to the present day as Scotland boasts the highest prison population per capita in Western Europe.

'The grave danger is that Scotland's parliament will be drowned in a sea of cynicism even before it gets off the ground,' concluded Jimmy Reid in 1999. As it turned out, this tide rose far less immediately than he expected, staved off at least in part by the 2014 independence Referendum. Nonetheless, today what little popular faith remains in the Scottish Parliament is at risk of being washed away.

Meanwhile, for Scotland's young people, everything changes, and everything stays the same. Tony Benn was right. Each generation must, indeed, fight the same battles again and again – including those born over the last 25 years. As this chapter's contributors explain, the devolution generation faces the challenge of a ballooning prison population, an education crisis and an energy transition – to name but a few. It is the future of these young people, many of whom were politicised by the question of Scotland's constitutional future, that this chapter aims to address.

In 2006, the Scottish poet Tom Leonard wrote that men and women were citizens of the world, 'responsible to that world and responsible for that world.' But by then, Leonard's commitment to humanity – and the importance of caring for one another – was out of fashion. Thatcherism and its ideological descendants saw to that. If, as Thatcher, argued, 'there [was] no such thing as society', then all that remained was the individual. Over decades, the social ties that once bound communities together were shattered by a concerted effort to pit neighbour against neighbour.

Atomisation followed as individuals, cut adrift from responsibility, were taught to look out for themselves. What Mark Fisher called 'magical voluntarism',

> the belief that it is within every individual's power to make themselves whatever they want to be

took root. People's powerlessness to resist falling living standards, for example, could be explained by the simple fact they weren't working hard enough. Questions of economics retreated from the political arena as neoliberalism's core tenets went unquestioned. People were denied the right to shape their destinies by an apparently immovable economic framework that instead empowered the market. Widespread apathy was the consequence.

In the 2024 General Election, just 47 per cent of voters turned out in Glasgow North East – the lowest anywhere in the city. Once the site of substantial heavy industry, areas like Springburn were decimated by deindustrialisation and never recovered. The Caley railworks, for example, closed as recently as 2019 after more than 140 years in business. Owned by the UK subsidiary of a German firm, it did not matter that the works were operating at a £4 million profit. They shut anyway. Couple this 40-year frustration with devolution's present stasis and the causes of alienation in Scotland today are evident.

Assessing this backdrop, the following chapter sets out to ask where Scotland is going. By taking three subject areas in turn, contributors interrogate the state of contemporary Scotland in order to unearth a path forward that learns the lessons of the last quarter century.

From Early Years through to Further Education, Andrea Bradley assesses the wrong turns and missteps taken in Scottish education. Laying out what measures need to be taken to fix these failures, she offers a route re-establishing the progressive educational journey that Scotland embarked upon in the early days of the Scottish Parliament.

Scotland's 'just' transition hangs in the balance, finds Rosie Hampton. Without detailed planning or significant state support, our energy transition risks failing both people and the planet. But it doesn't have to be this way. Hampton argues that with the combined power of the climate movement and organised labour, the energy transition can be reclaimed from corporate interests to deliver good, unionised, green jobs.

As questions of overcrowding in British prisons return to the headlines, Gavin Brewis traces a thread of Scottish moral panics to examine the criminalisation of working-class youth culture over the last three decades. Amidst a fresh wave of sensationalist news, he identifies a new and developing moral panic, arguing that it is high time for a different approach.

It is my hope that the following pages offer some insight as to whether the devolved settlement has, in fact, brought power closer to the people – and some instruction as to the work required of socialists, trade unionists and, critically, young Scots in the coming years. For it is they who face the task of correcting the faltering trajectory of the devolved settlement over the next 25 years.

Wisdom, Compassion, Justice, Integrity – the Promise for Education

Andrea Bradley

WITH THE OPENING of the Scottish Parliament in 1999, Scotland began a new journey as a country. Our destination, directions and landmarks? The values inscribed on the Scottish Parliament mace: wisdom, compassion, justice and integrity. These words still encapsulate where we should be going – our destination – and how we should be getting there – the routes that we take and how we travel – in all aspects of policymaking and implementation.

In regard to Scottish education, fully devolved, the journey began well. We put our best foot forward and made good headway in the early years.

A strong consensus formed around a new curriculum that promised a richer, fairer, more child-centred, inclusive and equitable educational experience for our youngest citizens from age 3–18. The Curriculum for Excellence (CFE) framework, predicated on professional trust, sought to empower Scottish teachers to create curricula bespoke to the needs of the learners in the school communities they served. Time and space would be freed up by lessening the high-stakes assessment load: breadth, depth, creativity and enjoyment of learning was promised for all learners – and their teachers – from nursery, where the early education begun by parents would be continued, through the stages of CFE right to s6.

No learner, regardless of any additional learning needs, would be left behind. In the early 2000s, in line with the values of CFE, the *Additional Support for Learning Act* was born, promising learners the right to have their needs assessed and recognised in the planning of all learning experiences offered by the education settings they attended – the presumption being that these would be mainstream settings, where all children would be wholly included, unless their needs were such that special education was a requirement.

In those nascent years of CFE, political party manifestos featured promises of class size reduction and some of those promises were even kept, at least in part.

A new millennium brought a new deal for Scotland's teachers, reflecting the hope that dawned with the inception of the new Parliament: in valuing education, Scotland would demonstrate that it strongly valued its teachers. *A Teaching Profession for the 21st Century,* aka The McCrone Agreement, committed to pay teachers a salary that more accurately reflected their worth as professionals, and to reducing and controlling workload through a 35-hour working week that included protected time for all teachers to prepare and mark – to design learning experiences and to provide learners meaningful feedback on their progress.

Here and now in 2024, Scottish education is still on a journey, but the directions and the signposts are harder to make sense of. We're making wrong turns and missteps. Neoliberal ideology has stalked the policymakers and at times lures them in the wrong direction, tempting some to believe that more for less is possible, indeed desirable, and that testing, targets, dashboards of data and league tables are how we keep committed, highly trained professionals on their toes. Rather, it puts and keeps them on their knees.

Class sizes in Scottish schools and the number of hours a week that teachers deliver lessons, with insufficient time to prepare and give feedback to students, continue to be amongst the highest of all OECD countries.

Meanwhile, the number of young people with recognised additional support needs has risen to 37 per cent – that's around 12 children per class of 30 or 33. The number of specialist ASN teachers has fallen, there aren't enough pupil support staff in schools, and the specialist services that sit outside of schools have been cut to the bone. The result? Teachers – and their students – are seriously struggling.

There are reams of evidence to show that teacher workload is out of control. The latest independent research commissioned by the Educational Institute of Scotland (EIS) highlights that teachers, on average, work more than 11 hours per week beyond the 35 hours that they're contracted, such are the demands upon them. In effect, teachers are subsidising the education system with unpaid labour, whilst thousands more qualified teachers are unemployed or under-employed on precarious contracts.

Scotland needs more teachers, yet teacher numbers are in decline. Whilst the Scottish Government and local authorities continue a long-running stand-off over the principle that teacher numbers matter, thousands of children with additional needs sit in classrooms unable to put pen to paper because they need help that can't come fast enough; or they sit outside the Headteacher's office waiting for a parent to arrive because they've been violent towards another child, teacher or member of support staff; or they sit at home because they can't face another day in school because of the worry and anxiety they feel, particularly post-pandemic, about being in a strained school environment. Data from the recent Scottish Government-commissioned Behaviour in Scottish Schools Research indicated upward trends in violent and aggressive behaviour amongst children in our schools. The steepest uptick is amongst children in p1 and p2. The findings of EIS research concur.

So how did we arrive here?

Quite simply, Scotland as a country isn't on the straightest road to addressing the impact of a decade and a half of austerity, compounded by the harms of the pandemic, followed by the ongoing cost of living crisis, all of which have wreaked the worst damage upon the poorest and most marginalised in our society and our school communities.

In such a trauma-rich socio-economic context, the importance of high-quality Early Years provision can't be overstated. There's a wealth of international research, including from the OECD, pointing to the need for governments to invest well in Early Years education, firmly featuring a play-based approach.

This is the best route to better outcomes for children cognitively, socially, and emotionally throughout their schooling, and to stronger employment and socio-economic outcomes, better physical and mental health outcomes, and more positive contributions to society, in adulthood.

A quick scan of the surroundings and one might think that Scotland is powering ahead on Early Years. The Scottish Government has a stated commitment to making Scotland the 'best place in the world to grow up' and giving children 'the best possible start in life.' With the extension of Early Learning and Childcare (ELC) entitlement to 1,140 hours for all three- and four-year-olds and vulnerable twos, it could be argued that the essential components are in place to realise the policy ambition. A careful look at the data, though, and the yawning gulf between policy and practice, resulting from insufficient investment and the decimation in the numbers of qualified teachers in the sector, is plain to see: there's been a 54 per cent reduction in the number of GTCS-registered teachers employed in ELC since 2010.

For almost a decade and a half, 3–5-year-olds have been short-changed to varying degrees, depending on where they live, by the current statutory provision which loosely promises only undefined 'access to a teacher'. The average nursery teacher to child ratio is 1:131. Since 2007, what was once a firm legal protection of our youngest children's entitlement to be taught by qualified teachers has all but gone and differing and ambiguous interpretations of 'teacher presence' and 'teacher access' continue to drive vast inequality of experience in early education across local authority jurisdictions.

An OECD Early Years study published in 2020, delivered a timely reminder and a stark warning to governments that early intervention measures, to support children's holistic development and address the gaps resulting from poverty and socio-economic disadvantage, are crucial in the strive for equity and in improving outcomes in later life:

> Starting behind means staying behind. When children's early learning is not strong before they start school and continues to be weak in the first two years of school, the outlook for these children is bleak.

We know the pandemic has wreaked the most damage upon children and families most disadvantaged by societal inequality, and that the achievement and attainment gap between children from the lowest income homes and those from the highest, continues.

So, while Scotland's investment in universally free early education and childcare reflects our grasp of the premise that early intervention matters, we still have a distance to travel towards the destination: quality, equitable early education, publicly funded and publicly delivered, including by sufficient numbers of qualified teachers.

Journeying through the Broad General Education (BGE) beyond Early Years, other hazards and hurdles are blocking the route to educational progress. Whilst the vision of CFE is 'permission-giving' of teachers to adopt creative approaches, the creativity it promised hasn't transpired for many young people in their primary and early secondary education. In large part, this is due to chronic under-resourcing and the persistence of a hierarchical, accountability culture – a neoliberal import – in the school system, which combine to undermine the capacity of teachers to develop and sustain the rich, personalised, learner-centred experiences promised by CFE.

CFE's four capacities – the enabling of young people to be successful learners, confident individuals, responsible citizens and effective contributors – are rightly lauded for their intention of realising the human right to education and preparing young people for democratic citizenship – something which, in today's world, can't be taken for granted.

In practice, though, the focus on the 'successful learner' predominates, with primary schools forced to place heaviest emphasis on Literacy and Numeracy attainment. In large part this is driven by the accountability demands of the Scottish Government's National Improvement Framework – a national data-gathering tool built to facilitate 'drilling down' into, and comparison of, the performance data of local authorities. Likewise, Science is prioritised to the detriment of creative and social subjects, as part of the wider promotion of 'stem' education – Science, Technology, Engineering and Maths – in pursuit of economic rather than wholly educational objectives – the neoliberal lure away from the broader and more essential human purposes of education.

Moreover, CFE's vision of trust in teacher professionalism and focus on learner-centred assessment has been undermined by the Scottish Government's introduction of computer-administered standardised assessments for all children at p1, p4, p7 and s3, in the face of widespread opposition from the teaching profession. Teachers would normally assess learning progress summatively when children are ready to be assessed, and assessments would be clearly linked to learning and next steps. EIS research, however, shows that, in the main, children are compelled to take these digital standardised tests regardless of their readiness, which is highly disruptive to teaching and learning. Further, most teachers deem the tests to be of little to no use at all in producing reliable information about learning and many express strong reservations about subjecting the youngest schoolchildren – four- and five-year-olds – to this assessment regimen. Whilst pleading poverty on many fronts, the Scottish Government has found millions of pounds to pay private companies for computerised standardised assessments and continues to do so every year, expecting schools to spend millions of hours of precious teaching time on their administration. This is money and time that could be much better spent taking us further and faster towards our intended destination.

Similarly, Scotland's vision of empowered teachers designing bespoke curricula in the interests of learners has been clouded by the pressure on school communities to respond to an array of national initiatives. That capacity is strained yet further in planning and assessing children's learning in the BGE, when teachers must navigate their way through literally hundreds of 'experiences and outcomes' and 'benchmark' statements. In need of a guide around the hazards and hurdles that block their way, Education Scotland provides teachers with less of a CFE route-map, and more of a maze.

The same is true of the Senior Phase – the stage of the learner journey between s4 and s6 – in which the design intention of CFE was that students would continue to learn across the four capacities, to experience breadth, depth, enjoyment and creativity in learning, and to undertake qualifications at an appropriate level, at an appropriate time, with formal assessment kept to an appropriate minimum.

The reality is again very different. An educationally anachronistic model of upper secondary education that originated in the 19th century, persists in 21st century Scotland, whereby our young people sit qualifications in every single year of the Senior Phase, with every qualification from National 5 to Advanced Higher featuring a formal examination. Scotland's young people are amongst the most examined in the developed world.

This three-year-long treadmill of course assessment and examinations diminishes the quality of the educational experience for Scotland's young people, as does the pressure on them and their teachers to acquire as many qualifications as possible, in a 'points make prizes' culture that sees schools and local authorities under pressure to compete with one another in the national accountability stakes. In this high-stakes, competitive environment, the young people who fare least well are those who are already the most disadvantaged by socio-economic inequality.

A recent independent review, commissioned by the Scottish Government, and undertaken by Professor Louise Hayward and a Review Group comprising members from all key stakeholder groups, offered Scotland a modern, fresh direction for the Senior Phase. The Scottish Government, with more than a year to consider the recommendations for progress, short of political courage and short of cash – in large part for reasons of its own making – has taken only baby-steps in the direction of a Senior Phase educational experience that Scotland could be proud of.

Beyond school education, the terrain we're crossing is also troubled and troubling.

Further Education colleges at the inception of devolution were inspiring and vibrant. They served the needs of communities – including new Scots – all across the country, teaching a broad range of courses.

The years that immediately followed saw political change for the sector, firstly in the welcome move to classification of colleges as public sector bodies. This brought governance changes designed to enable a focus on regional economic and skills needs. Regionalisation fuelled a reduction of 42 to 26 colleges, with mergers – fewer FE institutions rooted in their local communities. By 2015–16 over 40 per cent of all FE students were in Higher Education level courses, the highest ever. By 2018 FE students were being granted record levels of support through bursaries – very much a multi-directional journey.

The realisation of National Bargaining in 2014 was a cause for great optimism amongst FE lecturers, with salary, terms and conditions being equalised across the country. Another win was professional recognition for college lecturers through agreement with Scottish Government support, to enable lecturers' professional registration with the GTCS (General Teaching Council for Scotland).

Now, 25 years on from devolution, despite some gaining of ground, FE is off-track. A combination of funding crises, pressures to encourage private investment – in lieu of public funding and in return for a model of education provision bespoke to the needs of business above community – and flawed governance, have resulted in a decade's worth of industrial disputes that have exposed the failings of the sector. In the face of this, EIS-FELA (Further Education Lecturers Association) as the representative union of lecturers, has been forced to fight year after year to protect the jobs, salaries and conditions of lecturers, and the quality of community-centred education provision for students. Swathes of funding cuts have caused 1,700 lecturers, with a wealth of industry experience, to leave FE in round after round of voluntary severance in the last five years. The next two years promise more of the same.

One of the most notable trends since devolution has been the expansion of Higher Education. The number of students enrolling in Scottish universities has increased by around 25 per cent since 2014. The Scottish Government has maintained free tuition for Scottish-domiciled university students, paying student fees, whilst in other parts of the UK, students and their families foot the bill. One Scottish Government policy success through this expansion has been the significant increase in the number of students from socioeconomically poorer backgrounds gaining access to Higher Education.

On the face of it, then, Scotland is following a good path. Free tuition is a popular policy and is supported by the EIS. However, the Scottish Government's funding for HE teaching has fallen in real terms, and no longer covers the teaching costs for Scottish students. Non-UK students make up around a third of all enrolments in Scottish universities but contribute nearly three-quarters of the sector's total fee income – and cross-subsidise Scottish students' degrees. In some universities, Scottish students are in the minority as a result of the marketisation trends in play.

Whilst public funding for universities has fallen, their overall incomes have continued to grow due to international fees and research grants (for some universities). The need to recruit international students has led to significant capital projects to tempt prospective students and has resulted in a long-term squeeze on staff pay and pensions – both of which are negotiated at UK level, with no Scottish Government involvement.

The Scottish Government has tried to improve the lot of university staff to a greater extent than the UK Government – by putting pressure on Scottish universities to reduce zero-hours contracts and by championing Fair Work. However, neither initiative has really worked and the university sector in Scotland continues to employ large numbers of staff on casualised contracts to deliver its teaching. With a devolved collective bargaining context for Scottish universities and the trade unions that organise in the sector, arguably, much more ground could be made.

So, when it comes to education in Scotland, where are we and where are we going?

The teaching profession and the unions that represent teachers and lecturers, are still sure of the destination. Of that there's no doubt.

But every sector is facing difficult travel conditions, roadblocks and inadequately lit routes to progress. The vision from our policymakers isn't clear enough – not well enough articulated, not well enough connected to the way-finding values inscribed on the Parliament's mace, not well enough resourced.

But a few things *are* clear.

We have wayfinders on hand – a highly trained, skilled and professional education workforce, that despite the pull and sway of neoliberal crosswinds, and the increasing downwards pressure on public finances, has a firm hold of the moral compass that points to education as the route to individual improvement and social betterment – the common good. The vision and aims of policy in Scotland continue to lean true north – even by broad political consensus – but under-resourcing, somewhat driven by the neoliberal 'more for less' co-ordinates, are taking us somewhat off-course.

In short, the progressive educational journey that Scotland embarked on 25 years ago can't continue successfully without teachers and lecturers – the educationalists – showing the politicians the way, and our politicians accepting, and, crucially, trusting, that they require to be guided by those who know the destination, the route and the safest means of travel.

Twenty-five years on from devolution, the journey to wisdom, compassion, justice, and integrity in Scotland's education system is incomplete. But we must continue, keep looking up, eyes on the road, avoiding the hazards, keeping step, together. We will arrive.

Onwards...

Towards a Just Energy Transition

Rosie Hampton

SCOTLAND'S ENERGY TRANSITION sits at a crossroads. The opportunities of moving away from fossil fuels to genuinely renewable energy production are vast – yet they have to date been largely subsumed by the interests of capital, levied in the pursuit of private profit rather than moving towards a redistribution of wealth and control over our energy. The Scottish Government's approach so far has been to let this happen, quietly aiding and abetting the same energy companies that have increased their riches from the energy and cost of living crises, enabling them to reap the same reward from the energy transition. While it declares itself as a climate leader on the global stage, its actions ensure that none of the benefits of transition will remain in Scotland. And it shows no concern for the resources and working conditions of those in the Global South – who are simultaneously exploited by those private companies extracting wealth via supply chains that run from their countries to Scotland.

It does not have to be this way. Oil and gas workers in the North Sea, alongside their communities, have the experience and expertise to lead the transition away from fossil fuels. They know the ins and outs of the sector, and they are acutely aware of the barriers to moving into jobs in renewables. The path forward must be shaped by those workers and communities, lest we risk the same inequities of a privatised oil industry mapping onto our new energy system. We can instead, build something transformative.

In Scotland and across the UK so far, the market has dictated the pace and terms of the energy transition. The absence of any robust planning or investment to safeguard and secure the futures of workers in high-carbon industries has paved the way for wealthy, private companies to do as they please.

Nowhere is this more acutely demonstrated than in Grangemouth. In November 2023, Petroineos announced its plans to convert the refinery into an import and export terminal, axing the jobs of 500 workers across the site, in addition to many more across the supply chain and those indirectly employed by the refinery. The company is openly offshoring its carbon emissions for someone and somewhere else to deal with, dealing only with a fully refined imported product. At the time of the announcement, this would have been convenient for the Scottish Government too, as its targets only considered the emissions from *domestic* activities, rather than factoring in the total picture of consumption-based emissions from imported products and it has since scrapped those climate targets entirely. The decision to convert the refinery, with no transition plan, is abhorrent on climate, industrial, and moral grounds.

Three weeks after this announcement, Petroineos sought to assure the Scottish Government's Economy and Fair Work committee that there would be 'no change' in the product it would sell to its customers – a stark contrast in attitude when considering its refusal to give evidence to the same committee just three months earlier, on how it was developing plans for a just transition at the site. The company has continued to make it clear that it is happy for the refinery workers to be collateral damage, absorbing the shock of what Petroineos asserts is merely a commercial decision. An easy shorthand for the decimation of a town of skilled workers at the refinery and within the local community, who themselves have seen little of the benefits of Petroineos' £100 million yearly profits.

Yet it is hardly surprising that Petroineos has felt emboldened to act with impunity when it comes to the energy transition. The Scottish Government has been conspicuously absent, acting as a powerless stakeholder equally frustrated by the decisions of private energy companies. An unconvincing act in and of itself, it rings particularly hollow knowing that the Scottish Government was not hearing of the closure plans for the first time in November 2023. The proposals to shift the refinery to an import and export terminal were first put to Michael Matheson, then Cabinet Secretary for Net Zero, Energy, and Transport, in February 2022 – 18 months before Petroineos unilaterally announced the plans to the workers and the public. In that time, workers and the community of Grangemouth saw no tangible actions that would reassure them of the future of the plant. Whereas the company continued to receive public funding and grants from Scottish Enterprise, and from both the UK and Scottish governments in the form of Project Willow. With no conditionality attached to these grants – on job creation, transition plans, or targeted retraining for Grangemouth workers, for example – Petroineos continues to receive a free pass from both the Scottish and UK governments. Do as you please, take what you need is the message. From this perspective, the picture of Scotland's just transition from the top down looks bleak. If the Scottish and UK governments sit idly by while Petroineos leaves workers on the scrap heap in Grangemouth, it'll be no time at all before we see the same happen with other private energy companies across the sector.

Instead of investing in well-funded transition plans that create jobs in the immediate term, the Scottish Government is also wasting time actively considering expanding onshore oil and gas in Scotland, by considering SSE and Equinor's application to build a new gas-fired power station in Peterhead. The developers have promised that the plant will be fitted with the unproven, smokescreen technology that is carbon capture and storage (CCS), which has consistently over-promised and under-delivered across the globe. Eighty per cent of large-scale CCS projects have been either cancelled or put on hold, leaving workers in these projects in limbo as to whether their promised jobs will materialise. In Peterhead, the job figures estimated at the new power station represent a 30 per cent reduction in jobs compared to those at the existing plant – piercing the myth that CCS plants bring more jobs to any given area. What's more, SSE itself admits that 75 per cent of the construction jobs needed to build the new power station would go to people outside of the Aberdeenshire area. Hardly a just transition for the communities that have long scaffolded the oil and gas industry.

There can be an alternative. We can and should resist what Petroineos is doing in Grangemouth and stop it happening elsewhere, in the North East and beyond. The momentum behind a worker-led, grassroots movement for a just energy transition is growing. There is immense potential for transformative change, born from solidarity between workers and the climate movement, and a vision of a democratic, redistributive energy system where workers and their communities are the first to benefit from the transition, and the last to shoulder the cost.

To achieve this vision, it must be built from the first-hand expertise and experience of workers and communities who have worked in and have supported the offshore and onshore energy sector to date. No one knows the ins and outs of the energy sector like those working within it. Many oil and gas workers enact the move to renewables at the everyday level, working between rigs and offshore wind farms on different contracts. Consequently, the barriers to transitioning are not an abstract idea. They are felt in the terms and conditions of workers in oil and gas in real time. If any boss is able to hide behind a smokescreen of being a 'green' employer in renewables, while still enacting the same exploitation of their workers, we will lose the argument around a just transition.

As an example, it is inarguable that offshore oil and gas workers have the transferable skills to be the first to work in renewables. Yet workers still regularly have to pay out of their own pocket for training costs that would enable them to transfer easily across sectors and work safely. As revealed in the Platform Report, *Public Ownership of Energy Generation in North East Scotland* (2023), many workers pay upwards of £2,000 of their own money on updating their training, with employers regularly making zero contribution to training costs. If employers and the Scottish and UK governments take this approach to the retraining needed for workers to move to renewables, they are offloading the cost of the transition onto workers and communities who have worked in and supported the oil and gas industry for decades already. There is nothing 'just' about that.

We need to see tangible measures such as a ring-fenced funding package to support retraining and job creation, to veer away from this laissez-faire approach to the transition. Putting workers at the heart of the energy transition is morally just, but it also needs to lead to material benefits for those workers and communities involved. There is no more time for warm words and endless consultations that pay lip service to the demands of organised workers and their communities. The asks have not changed. More advisory boards, government inquiries, industry meetings, and focus groups will not advance the transition to renewable energy. It's about acting upon the wealth of knowledge and experience that already exists. For the energy transition to be just, it needs to revolve around trade union- and worker-led transition plans that are shaped to the needs and the future of the sector.

The plans for the energy transition must simultaneously be underpinned by public ownership and public control. Instead of leaving the energy transition in Grangemouth and across Scotland to private companies, the Scottish Government could take transformative action around energy ownership and generation. Local public ownership of local generation can play a significant role in ensuring substantial numbers of jobs are actually created. It is estimated in *Our Power* that the North East of Scotland could benefit from 27,000 new jobs in genuinely clean energy, if each stage of energy generation was publicly owned in Scotland. Private generation and financing of energy is already heavily dependent on public money, including through subsidies. Increasing public spending but keeping it within public control at national, local, and community level would mean that we retain a say over how the benefits of the energy transition are distributed – by investing in jobs in local, green industries, and reinvesting back into crucial public services.

Simultaneously, this must be rooted in a global just transition, that accounts for how the resources we need for the transition are acquired. Transition minerals, such as lithium and steel, are vital to the energy transition away from fossil fuels. While Scotland must transform its energy systems to meet its climate goals, to do so without minimising demand for transition minerals will compromise the aims of the transition and risk failing to deliver a renewable energy system. We need a system-wide reckoning with how the move to renewables impacts on other countries where these minerals are present. Scotland already has a responsibility as a historic polluter to do more and to enact due diligence towards those workers in the Global South in the transition mineral supply chain, where human rights and labour abuses, environmental destruction and rampant exacerbation of climate injustice are endemic. Scotland's energy transition will not only be made here. When we call for justice for workers, it must be for all workers across the supply chain, particularly in the Global South. To stand with workers in the energy transition means ensuring our solidarity is global, and not limited to national boundaries.

Organising for a just energy transition in Scotland and across the globe cannot be left solely to the workers in those sectors. A coalition between workers, trade unions, community groups, and climate groups represents the political dynamite needed to reignite the energy transition. A climate movement that is clear on the industrial policies and measures needed to support the transition leaves no room for the market to pretend their concerns are about anything other than protecting their bottom line. If we're able to argue for a windfall tax on oil and gas companies with one hand, whilst demanding ring-fenced, substantial investment into job creation and training with the other, there is no ambiguity regarding who *actually* stands with oil and gas workers.

The task moving forward is to reclaim the energy transition from the market and place the power firmly back in the hands of workers. We've got to stand, as workers and communities across the world, across the climate movement and the trade unions, demanding that our governments turn the tide of the energy transition, away from the market and towards the people. In the first *Red Paper on Scotland,* the collection opened with these musings by Gordon Brown:

> We suggest that the real resources of Scotland are not the reserves of oil beneath the sea (nor the ingenuity of native entrepreneurs) but the collective energies and potential of our people, whose abilities and capacities have been stultified by a social system which has for centuries sacrificed social aspirations to private ambitions.

The same words that rang true at the discovery of oil are pertinent to its decline. The transition to renewable energy could be one of *re*-industrialisation for Scotland, that brings good, unionised, secure jobs to workers in the North East and beyond, supporting communities who have long been the last to see the benefits of a privatised oil and gas industry. Reclaiming the energy transition for the people is the task of our time and it will happen – not by politicians' goodwill, but from an organised labour movement and climate movement in Scotland and beyond.

Moral Panics – Criminalising Young People

Gavin Brewis

GLASGOW HAS A 'schizophrenic' character. Perhaps not the most politically correct statement from the 2010 book by Carol Craig, *The Tears that Made the Clyde: Well-Being in Glasgow*, but one which few scholars who study Glasgow and its history of crime and violence would disagree with. Despite the supposed success of the 'Glasgow's Miles Better' Campaign in the 1980s in improving its image, socio-spatial inequality would continue to plague the working-class areas of the city. By the 1990s, amid fresh concerns around gangs, violence, and a new folk devil in Ned Culture, Scotland began construction of its first private prison in Kilmarnock. This essay will explore the impoverished economic conditions through which Neds emerged, and the intersections of private prisons and the criminalisation of this working-class youth culture, which led to a range of discriminatory public policies, and a sharp increase in the prison population. As the new Labour Government raise concerns around prison overcrowding, and problematic young people, this essay will provide a fresh perspective into previous attempts to address these similar – and cyclical – issues for Glasgow.

From 'Hooligans' (1906) and 'Gangsters' (1930s) to the 'Teddy Boys' and 'New Hooliganism' (1950–1970s), Glasgow has been no stranger to moral panic throughout time. Though, with a sharp decline in demand for heavy industry from the first decade of the 20th century, and a mismanaged and 'reckless' deindustrialisation from the 1970s, the crime and criminalisation of such youth cultures did not occur as coincidence but as a direct consequence of poverty and inequality. By the 1980s, due to this long-standing reputation of the city as dangerous and impoverished, Glasgow City Council set out to reshape the narrative. One of the first cities in Europe to operationalise Thatcher's neoliberal agenda, Glasgow introduced its regeneration project through the 'Glasgow's Miles Better' Campaign (1984). Indeed, the promotion was successful in some ways, creating inward revenue through finance capital and by hosting a number of international events. For example, in 1988, the city held the prestigious Garden Festival and was awarded the title of the European City of Culture just two years later in 1990. The city came to boast an impressive £2.5 billion worth of investment, which was put to work on infrastructure and cleansing, while employment soared from 94,000 to 158,000. But while the city had improved in parts, the socio-spatial inequality which had existed since the inception of capitalism was to continue.

New money may have been flowing through the economy, but this was generated via low wages, and only just enough to survive on, given that the National Minimum Wage did not yet exist. Furthermore, events such as the Garden Festival and Glasgow Alive, had only paid workers on seasonal and temporary contracts, and so had minimal impact on the lasting overall issue of joblessness. While there were some efforts at maintenance for parts of the less affluent estates such as the Gorbals and Pollok, most of the new money available was spent on improving Glasgow aesthetically, or on projects that could support further economic growth such as the Clyde Waterfront Regeneration. By 1998, Scotland's child poverty rates were as high as 28 per cent, both in absolute and relative terms. And, while there may have been a steady decline from 1999, Glasgow's figures around this issue remained particularly high. Coincidentally, across the latter half of the decade, stories had begun to develop around a new problem of 'gangs', an apparent phenomenon that was conveniently never accompanied with a fixed definition. Areas which would face the greatest level of negative attention were those of the least affluence. Working-class areas – places with existing spatial discredit – would find themselves central to what was essentially a growing panic. Of course, with the regeneration project still ongoing – this attempt to change Glasgow's image – there was an initial reluctance to sensationalise the issue. In fact, success stories of the former Easterhouse Project, and improvements in tackling crime, were printed across the media until the latter half of the 1990s to present this issue as something long gone. This was despite the fact that in 1995, Glasgow was to experience six murders in a single weekend.

By 1997 the narratives around gangs had intensified and by the end of the decade, an old but repurposed term became commonplace throughout the newspapers; that of the Ned. The shift occurred just as the foundations were laid for Scotland's first private prison in Kilmarnock, a long-standing neoliberal project. Kilmarnock was part of a Private Finance Initiative (PFI), a Public Private Partnership (PPP) scheme introduced by the UK Government that saw the financing, building, and operating of public infrastructure, such as prisons, hospitals, and schools, while the Government compensated the private companies over a long-term contract. Tony Blair's Labour Government came into power in May 1997, and just six months later, the Scottish Office agreed that Premier Prisons would be awarded the contract. Premier was a joint venture between the American private prison operator Wackenhut Corrections Corporation and a British facilities management firm, Serco PLC. The prison opened in 1999, a few months after Scottish devolution, and was immediately covered in controversy. The use of private prisons was already questionable but, following a report in *The Guardian* which had shown how Jack Straw, the UK Home Secretary, had awarded Premier the Doncaster Prison contract against advice from civil servants, further suspicions were raised.

Kilmarnock had been an unmitigated disaster, with Premier cutting costs and struggling to employ capable staff members. The Scottish Parliament Justice Committee reported in 2002 that this was largely because of the low wages on offer. Furthermore, the company would go on to boast a poor record of rehabilitation due to the lack of opportunities and qualifications on offer inside the prison. The SNP challenged these issues almost from the outset, revealing how Premier had made around £1 million in profits over the space of two years, £700,000 of which had come from public funds. The debate around private prisons became somewhat lost in petty politics, with Labour fighting to promote their benefits, and the SNP doing the opposite. Nonetheless, it was clear by this point that the public were not in favour of these prisons, and their reputation had worsened as a consequence of Kilmarnock's failures. But despite public support for private prison schemes being at an all-time low, by 2002, politicians began venting their concerns around the overcrowding of prisons, and it was announced that three new private prisons were planned for Scotland.

The following year, the First Minister, Jack McConnell announced his 'War on Neds'. By this time, Ned had become something of a buzzword. Due to its fluid definition, it could be utilised as and when its user saw fit. Emphasis was placed particularly on Glasgow, as homicide figures had increased the year prior. Interestingly, 2002 saw nine fewer murders than 1995, but of course, at that time, there was still a bid by Glasgow's city council to encourage investment and portray the city as having conquered its long-standing issue with criminality. It was also obvious from the reporting that the term Ned had been used interchangeably with that of 'gang member', which in itself was a limitation given there was no fixed definition of what that actually meant. Still, the moral panic around this youth culture provoked sensationalism, as the Scottish Executive worked hand in hand with the *Daily Record,* who assisted them in asking the public what *they* wanted done about these 'Neds'. The 'responses' published by the *Daily Record* resulted in what could be expected from an outlet perpetuating panic. There were calls for tagging, national service, microchipping, and violence from the police against such 'Neds'. Of course, the identities of the contributors were never revealed beyond their first name and profession. Teachers, surgeons and even police officers had allegedly written in to vent their disgust at this rising problem. As the letters were never made public it is impossible to say if these comments were an accurate reflection of all responses.

Some months later, the Scottish Government would introduce the *Antisocial Behaviour etc. (Scotland) Act 2004*, which was in many ways the political legitimisation of this now growing panic. The Act allowed new powers for the state to introduce electronic tagging of children, orders obliging parents to tame 'unruly children', and measures to tackle noisy neighbours and graffiti. The most concerning rulings, though, were the introduction of the ASBO for children as young as 12, and the Dispersal Order. According to the Order, groups of 'two or more people' causing alarm or distress could be dispersed – what was causing alarm or distress was entirely subjective and at an officer's discretion. This was particularly apparent in part three of the Order, where it stated that in specific instances, 'police can arrest a person without warrant'. Thus, police were given a power that was hitherto unknown, and it was to be exercised, in line with the Antisocial Behaviour Act, in areas with histories of 'antisocial behaviour' – perhaps better described as working-class areas with an existing spatial discredit.

With these new laws in place, crime figures would inevitably rise. Glasgow had become renowned for its harsh sentences around violence and weapon-carrying, with first-time offenders often given custodial sentences. Of course, Glasgow was not without its flaws and was dubbed by the BBC the 'Murder Capital of Europe' in 2005. This was despite the fact that the number of homicides in the city had been higher in both 2002 and in 1995, and of the 137 murders across Scotland, only six had been carried out by a rival gang member; again, this term was used by statisticians without definition. Nonetheless, with these figures and the moral panic around Neds, alongside this new title of the 'Murder Capital', the letters that continued to pour into the *Daily Record* demanded harsher and longer sentences for this problematic subculture at a time when prisons were apparently filling up. Therefore, when it was announced that the new private prison in Addiewell was to begin construction in 2006, public opinion had been altered significantly, and the news was in many ways celebrated. This was in spite of the obvious concerns around the first private prison, Kilmarnock, which by now had been shown by an undercover BBC reporter in a 2005 programme *Private Prison Failings Exposed*, to be neglecting and even abusing vulnerable prisoners, while falsifying mandatory suicide watchlists documents. Built between Glasgow and Edinburgh, in a former village once renowned for its industry, Addiewell would, like many other private prisons, come to occupy a space once reserved for industry and labour, in an area of deprivation, addiction and crime, that had worsened as a consequence of deindustrialisation.

By the time the SNP came to form a minority government in 2007, Scotland was to see a decline in violent crimes and murder. In fact, since taking power, no new private prisons have been built in Scotland, despite the plans by the previous Government. Some authors have addressed this sudden reduction in crime, attributing it to the important work of the Scottish Violence Reduction Unit, and a positive aspect of 'Scottish exceptionalism' in how the violence was to be understood. Indeed, the evidence on this is difficult to contest, but it is possible that there is further analysis to be made. Because with the end of Labour in Scotland, also came an end to the panic, and Scotland's ambitions around private prisons. In fact, on the face of it, the SNP were to take a far less conservative approach to youth crime in general. This was not just around the language, as can be seen by their decision to put into law considerations around the brain development of offenders under the age of 25. Indeed, while much can be said about the SNP's neoliberal policies which may affect such young people in other ways, particularly within Glasgow which still struggles desperately with child poverty, private prisons are something they are yet to adopt. Figures reveal that since 1990, Scotland's prison population has risen by 60 per cent. The sharpest rise in the population occurred almost entirely under Scottish Labour during this moral panic. Though, while there was an initial decline in prisoners under the SNP, figures in recent years have once again risen. In fact, Scotland now boasts the highest prison population per capita in Western Europe (136 per 100,000).

Recent months have seen fresh cries over prisons as overcrowded, while the country faces a new developing moral panic around its young people. Although crime figures have risen somewhat, there is much to be said about the potential re-weaponising of this issue. Subjective documentaries and one-sided, sensationalist newsreels are once again becoming commonplace around this supposedly growing problem. A similar pattern also ensued after the 2024 General Election saw the Conservative Government replaced by Labour, who also won by a landslide in Scotland. The implications of this are not yet clear, but it is important to recognise this developing trend, and to remain conscious over moral panic being deliberately whipped up to – potentially – further an economic agenda.

Of course, much of what has been stated in this essay may very well be coincidence. Perhaps the prisons filled naturally, and the War on Neds did not encourage moral panic. Maybe the Antisocial Behaviour Act (2004) did not play a role in worsening the figures around crime. It may very well be that the population of youth in the early 2000s were simply the worst version of youth that the country has ever seen. Worse than the early 1900s; worse than the 1930s; worse than the 1970s; worse than anything that had gone before, but indeed, perhaps not quite as problematic as the dangerous new trends of youth in the present, who may very well be, the worst of all...

Politics Through Culture

Introduction

Denise Christie

IMAGINE STANDING IN the heart of Glasgow, surrounded by the vibrant sounds of street performers and the spirited chatter of diverse voices. As you stroll through the city, you can't help but feel the pulse of a culture rich in history and resilience. In 2025, Scotland is not just a backdrop for political debates; it is a living tapestry woven from the threads of art, music, and activism. But how did we arrive at this moment? What stories lie beneath the surface of our cultural landscape?

In 1975, *The Red Paper on Scotland* emerged as a bold manifesto for socialism and nationalism during a Labour Government era. While it addressed political and economic themes, it largely overlooked the cultural dimensions that shape our identities. This omission highlights how culture was once an afterthought in political discourse but has since become a central pillar.

Fast forward to 2000, and another Labour Government oversaw significant changes with the reconvening of the Scottish Parliament in 1999. This marked a pivotal moment in Scotland's political landscape, reflecting a shift towards greater autonomy and recognition of Scotland's unique cultural identity.

The first chapter in this section, 'Politics and Struggle in Film', invites us to reflect on this evolution through the lens of grassroots filmmaking and feminist activism. Authors Núria Araüna Baró and David Archibald challenge us to amplify voices that have been historically silenced, emphasising that true solidarity transcends borders and economic metrics. They highlight grassroots filmmaking as a tool for fostering international solidarity and cultural exchange, particularly through projects connecting feminist activists across Cuba and Scotland.

Susan Morrison's chapter transports us back to a time when theatre was a powerful vehicle for social change. This era was characterised by unapologetically left-wing theatre companies like Wildcat and 7:84, which used their platforms to challenge societal norms and address issues of class and identity. Imagine young audiences captivated by productions that tackled class struggles head-on, providing a voice to the working class while igniting conversations that still resonate today.

It's not just theatre that has shaped our cultural identity; but as Tommy Breslin and I try to describe, music has played an equally transformative role. 'The Resonance of Music: A Catalyst for Change' explores how melodies and lyrics have served as rallying cries for social justice throughout history. From the anthems of Two Tone to contemporary artists like Young Fathers, music continues to unite us in our shared struggles and aspirations. This chapter also shines a light on the persistent barriers women encounter in the music industry and those sisters leading the charge to dismantle these barriers.

Finally, 'Take it Back to the Centre?' offers a reflective narrative on football's cultural significance in Scotland. It examines how football serves as both a unifying force and a potential distraction from pressing social issues. Julie McNeill's chapter discusses football's deep roots in working-class communities and its role in providing support where politics often falls short. It raises critical questions about national identity and the potential for sport to both unite and divide societies. Picture yourself in a packed stadium, where cheers for your team echo alongside calls for social justice. Football is not merely a game; it is a reflection of our collective hopes and frustrations. McNeill's poetry brilliantly captures why football resonates so deeply with so many people.

Reflecting on 25 years since the reconvening of the Scottish Parliament, we see its achievements in shaping modern Scottish politics. The Parliament has played a crucial role in addressing issues unique to Scotland, fostering legislative changes that reflect its distinct cultural identity.

The 2014 independence referendum was another significant milestone, fundamentally impacting Scotland's political dynamics. It sparked ongoing debates about independence and devolution, influencing both political discourse and cultural expression.

Looking ahead we speculate on Scotland's evolving cultural identity and political landscape. With ongoing discussions about independence and devolution, what future can we envisage when we listen to all our stories? How will diverse voices continue to shape Scotland's narrative?

Together, these chapters weave a rich narrative that invites us to reconsider what it means to be Scottish in today's world. As we navigate this new era filled with challenges and opportunities, let us embrace the diverse voices that shape our understanding of culture and identity. These authors encourage readers to reflect on their own experiences while setting the stage for deeper exploration of the themes presented in this collection. What future can we imagine when we listen to all our stories?

Culture and That

Susan Morrison

IT'S A FAIRLY safe bet that when *The Red Paper on Scotland* made its first appearance in 1975, I wouldn't have read it. In fact, I doubt very much that I would even have heard of it. In my defence, I was only 15 and my 'O' levels and Highers were taking up most of my time. We were doing *Macbeth*, and so Miss Brown of the English department arranged that we should visit the Citizens Theatre in Glasgow to see the new production on stage.

It's just as well we went before the review in *The Scotsman*. The play kicked off with a

> blast of electronic rock music… with the lights blinking and flickering and the band perched up on battlements making a mighty noise… all it amounts to is a kind of Dunsinane Disco. The witches, who might at first be mistaken for the Wombles of Wimbledon, are transformed.

At the end MacDuff chucked a heap of offal on the stage with a sickening splash:

> [Macbeth] appears to have been disembowelled instead of beheaded and, considering the horrible mess that has been made of the play, it is an appropriate fate

This is all before we also found out that Hecate, Queen of the Witches, made her grand entrance in the bare scud. Miss Brown was outraged and wrote a strongly worded letter of complaint to the legendary Giles Havergal, who probably ignored it. The fifth years, without exception, loved it. Particularly the boys.

The Citizens Theatre of the late 1970s will always be a touchstone of Scottish culture. It was the first grown up place I went to without adult supervision. My pal Anne and I went religiously, and watched everything. Every ticket was 50p a pop. It was open to all, and you could see that.

It sat squat in the middle of tower blocks and tenements. You could watch the lights in the living rooms go out and see people cross the road to join the queue. It was, and is, a source of pride to the people of the Gorbals.

It was a theatre rooted in its community, but with an audience that came from the entire city. It was classless. Folk from the concrete towers across the way sat next to the 'wally close' people, the sort who bought chicken bricks from Habitat.

Some plays were baffling, but it didn't matter. If you didn't fully grasp what Giles was doing, there was the spectacle to watch, the joy of being in an audience and, anyway, there would be something else next month. And there was always the Christmas panto, which was quite unlike anything else in the city.

At the same time as the Citz, we had touring productions by companies that were unapologetically left-wing. Wildcat, the word the right-wing press used for unofficial strike action, gave us *Confessin' The Blues*, a musical comedy about love, marriage, and sex. Given that Scotland was still suffering a Calvinist hangover at the time, the fact that they made it funny was remarkable. They also brought us *The Steamie*, a stone-cold classic of working-class life.

7:84 must be the only theatre company ever named after a statistic, and a damming one at that. Seven cent of the population own 84 per cent of the wealth. It's probably worse now. They gave us the magnificent *The Cheviot, the Stag and the Black, Black Oil*, the tale of the historic sellout of Scotland's assets. It was grimly funny:

It begins, I suppose, with 1746 – Culloden and all that. The Highlands were in a bit of a mess.

When we got older, pubs everywhere in Glasgow seemed to be booming with live music. Punk still had an influence. Anyone could pick up a guitar or a pair of drumsticks and hammer the living daylights out of it. Yes, most of it was terrible, but some went on to greater things, trained in those sticky-floored pubs.

It was all furious, loud and funny, and the only places we regularly heard ourselves being performed.

We rarely appeared on our television screens. The big soap opera of the day was set in Manchester, the comedies had the accents of Surbiton and Surrey, occasionally Newcastle. Dramas tended to go for more southern accents. Even children's television was presented by lovely people who couldn't find Pittenweem on a map and had a dreadful habit of smiling into the camera to say 'If you're in London this weekend...'. There would be an exhibition at the British Museum or a ship moored on the Thames. Just pop up to London. No, not you, North of the Border.

In the great mass of cultural media, we were firmly second-class. Sure, there were the glittering exceptions – *The Vital Spark*, *Sutherland's Law* and, later, *Tutti Frutti* – but they never seemed to last long. What did last was the Cringe.

They'd land it on us at Hogmanay, usually. There would be comedy sketch shows. Quite a lot about football. Some of it would be funny. Fortunately, only we saw them. And then they'd go network for the Bells and bring out the big guns of twee tartan dancers, endless bloody fiddle music, and Fran 'n' Anna, a pair of plaid-swathed pansticked sisters from Coatbridge. They usually wore fishnet tights and mini-kilts. Scotland was Brigadoon hatching into life under the glare of the television lights.

The great, mad, boiling mass of theatre, music and literature of Scottish culture outside those walls was hardly acknowledged. Our own television media was mildly obsessed with sport, gardening shows and Andy Stewart. There were two attempts at urban soaps. *High Living*, set in a Glasgow tower block, and *Garnock Way*, the story of a mining village. They only lasted about three years each. Neither made it to national channels. It was felt that the grit of the cities was too much for our more tender middle-class cousins, who could apparently handle *Coronation Street*. No, a story of misty lochside glens with Highland accents was considered much more appropriate, and so *Take the High Road* appeared.

It was all part of a steady, managerial and dangerous categorisation of our culture into neat little boxes, ranked in order of 'significance', weighted by what was considered marketable. The romantic was promoted. Scotland's traditional arts of music, storytelling and dance had the harsh edges of their beginnings in taverns, ceilidhs and stramashes carefully smoothed away and re-engineered as something far more seemly. The sort of thing you'd imagine in the TV adaptation of a Jane Austen novel. Anyone who has actually seen a ceilidh in all its full-throated fury will know that it's more of a contact sport than a gentle quadrille.

The industrial working class was quietly ignored. Well, urban decay was a tougher sell than tartan and white heather.

To aid this stratification, arts management as a career really gained traction in the '80s. You could do courses in it. Very pleasant people, usually with the accents of Hampstead and Islington, started to appear in venues and institutions. They would listen intently with their heads tilted at roughly 35 degrees to one side.

They rose. Many of them wound up on the very peaks of Scottish cultural life. They ran things, that gave out money and were terribly polite. They brought with them their cultural background, and very little was working class. Too gritty, mate. What we need here is something avant garde. *The Observer* will love it. To be fair, they were just as damaging in the North of England.

Let's be honest, no one ever likes the holders of the purses, especially if they don't get that funding they asked for. But in the next few decades the biggest funder of all, the Arts Council Scotland, later Creative Scotland, stood repeatedly accused of a middle-class bias. And it's hard to say that's not true when you grant £86,000 in funding to a show which involved 'non-simulated' sex. What would Miss Brown have made of that?

I speak from a personal perspective here, since I work at the cultural coalface, but in an art form that is routinely dismissed as 'just' comedy. In the rarefied world of 'arts management', laughter of itself is regarded with serious side-eye. Humour may be deployed, but only in the safe settings of frightfully amusing re-imagining of classical works, something whimsical in a gallery or a dance piece that raises a thin smile from the cognoscenti. Stand-up comedy is the snotty-nosed kid in the corner. What possible artistic merit can there be in creating, editing and performing on a stage with sweary words and knob jokes? Too low-brow. Unless Joe Orton wrote it.

I suspect the funders think that stand-up comedy is easy. It is. It's like doing a triple-double back salto tucked with a triple twist. If you're Simone Biles.

Oddly, an astonishing number of Scottish comedians are from working-class backgrounds. It's probably something to do with its accessibility.

It is vital to reflect an entire nation in our culture, particularly the ones for whom our society and its structures are just not working. The zero-hours contracted, the minimum wagers, the workless and the carers. Only when we hear them do we try to put things right. Well, some of us at any rate. But right now young performers and artists are being denied places to learn and grow. The staggering burden of student loans puts places like The Royal Conservatoire of Scotland and the Edinburgh College of Art beyond the reach of the working-class kids. All over Scotland live music venues are closing. Communities are trying to take halls and small theatres into local ownership, just to keep the stages open for performers, but the bell keeps tolling the same dull message – there is no money.

We've been here before. When Thatcher launched her cold war on Scotland's industries in the '80s, there was even less money. But there was an older working class that had once seen itself on the stage, page and screen, and fought hard with sheer bloody mindedness to survive. Those theatre companies piled props into vans that only just made it through the MOT and hit the halls of the Highlands and Islands, the cities and the Borders. There were kids out of Easterhouse and Lochee who formed bands and honed their skills in those smoky pubs in Dundee and Glasgow. Young artists were trained in our colleges and art schools.

We need to grow this creativity. There is no 'no money'. There is some money. There must be. We can afford bombs, and they're not cheap. Let's get some grassroots growth going. Protect the venues, open the access to the learning, get them on stages. Obviously, I draw the line at providing young people with mechanically dangerous transit vans.

Let's make sure it reaches beyond those who have the Bank of Mum and Dad behind them. We need the diversity, if only to avoid a future of a tourist-trap Scotland shrouded in tartan endlessly serenaded at Hogmanay by a re-animated Fran 'n' Anna.

When Burns wrote 'wad some Power the giftie gie us / To see oursels as others see us!' it was as a warning to those cocksure of themselves, but take out those last four words, and you're left with 'to see oursels'. Culture gives us the power to see ourselves. We can see who we are in the mirrors of music, art and performance.

The rising generations are suffering from record levels of mental illness, and some of that is to do with isolation. Doors once open to us are closing in their faces. If young people don't see or hear themselves in the cultural media around them, how can they feel they have a stake in it? If they have no stake in the culture their society produces, why should they care about the community that creates that culture? It's not theirs.

Bugger it. Let's buy a van and hit the high road.

Politics and Struggle in Film

David Archibald & Núria Araüna Baró

FROM THE VANTAGE point of 2025, there are several striking features of *The Red Paper on Scotland 1975*. For the purposes of this essay, and in line with our interests as socialists and feminists working in Film and Media Studies within higher education, we will begin with two.

Firstly, it is notable that none of the essays focus primarily on questions of culture. This says something, of course, about the 1970s; but it also says something about the present. Now that a similar collection of essays is being assembled in 2025, it is inconceivable that questions of culture would not occupy a more central position. To be fair to the 1975 edition, cultural matters are present, if not dominant, in Tom Nairn's essay *Old Nationalism and New Nationalism*; however, much of the book focuses on history, economics and constitutional matters. Since the '70s, cultural production has become synonymous with economic production, something which seems to have legitimised its public importance within neoliberal discourse: for example, in 2021, Screen Scotland noted that over 10,000 workers were employed in a sector which added £627m to the Scottish economy, and recently announced a target of £1 billion for the latter. Culture, moreover, has also become an increasingly dominant aspect of political life and political discourse.

A second striking feature is that the 27 essays and short introduction contained in *The Red Paper* are all written by men. Written political analysis, at least for the book's editor, seems to have been something of a boy's game.

Our interests are different: we are interested in culture, although not primarily from an economic perspective; and we are interested in women's voices. For the last few years, we have been developing an alternative, grassroots approach towards filmmaking. Our contribution is modest: we do what we can where we are, whilst contributing to the building of alternative international networks of support and solidarity. For example, we are involved with the Radical Film Network, an international network of academics, activists and filmmakers, and in local struggles for social justice. Initially, through the production of *Comrades together-apart/Camarades junts-i-a-banda* (2021), which we shot on phones in our respective home cities (Vilanova i la Geltrú and Glasgow) and edited together at distance, we explored how audiovisual technologies might be utilised by political activists and politically engaged academics to foster conversations at distance. In the making of this short film, which featured images of political struggles in Catalunya and Scotland, we explored how these technologies could be used to share a sense of place and time, and to foster what we have termed 'alliancial thinking', which can, in turn, help develop alliance building.

With a small grant from within the university sector, in October 2022 we commenced a collaborative research project with Havana Glasgow Film Festival (HGFF) which widened this project beyond our own reach. We aimed to connect feminist activists in four historically related cities – Havana (Cuba), which is twinned with Glasgow, and Matanzas (Cuba), which is twinned with Vilanova i la Geltrú – to explore how no- and low-budget filmmaking might be utilised to build connections with the participants, weaving trans-local alliances through audiovisual means, building networks of support and solidarity amongst feminist activists and collectives.

Rather than viewing culture on economic terms, our focus is on how it might be put to use. For example, instead of twinning agreements based on a colonial historical past materialised by men in suits travelling between cities to discuss trade or tourism, we sought to connect grassroots feminists through creativity. By developing a cross-cultural project rooted in specific patriarchal states, labelled as capitalist and communist, the project amplifies the often-unheard voices of non-state actors with the aim of developing how life could be made more liveable through thinking around what Catalan philosopher Marina Garcés has termed '*un món comú*' (a common world).

Feminism is the long fight for gender equality, and yet, a term that has acquired many different meanings. It means different things in Cuba, Catalunya and Scotland, and its nuances and approaches differ for many people within these same geographies. As bell hooks notes, feminism has also been wielded as a tool to legitimise imperialist, colonial aggressions, such as, we might add, Israel's genocidal acts in Gaza. There is, then, a struggle over the present and future definition of 'feminist' and of the feminist movement itself, and many voices demand feminisms that are concerned with the multiple axis of oppression that intersect with gender inequality.

In one notable act in 2022, activists in Havana and Matanzas recorded short video messages addressed to Victor, a young Catalan man facing three years in prison for his part in disrupting the far right on the streets of Barcelona. In this act, solidarity emerged as an embodied, physical, experience, and an intellectual one. The video message was received enthusiastically and shared widely on social media across Catalunya, provoking a sense of surprise and warmth towards this remote yet close connection; a sense that even with words having different meanings in both contexts ('*solidaridad*', '*antifascista*', 'repression'), translations could foster new ways of supporting each other's human rights. It was an early example of how the audiovisual process of production might foster mutually supportive trans-local dialogues, which were in line with our own dialogical approach to filmmaking.

We subsequently secured further funding and over the last two years, feminists from the four cities have developed a series of short films. Notably, in December 2023, four work-in-process films made by the activists were presented at the Festival Internacional del Nuevo Cine Latinoamericano de La Habana (International Festival of New Latin American Cinema of Havana) alongside a festival symposium under the heading 'cine dialógico' (dialogical cinema), which is the name that the Cuban participants gave to the project. The screened films were *Acariciar la vida*, *Pasos a una mirada trans*, *Pegadas a mi alma*, and *The Hands Film (untitled)*.

In the production of these films, and in the ongoing projects that the activists are making, the participants offer their voices, but also seek others whose voices will be listened to, in the process of filmmaking, in the film itself, and in the film's exhibition. Listening to these voices emerge in multifarious form opens a pathway to develop alliancial thinking with the participants themselves, with audiences in the four cities, and, we hope, beyond.

There is no shortage of critiques of audiovisual technologies and their (often extreme right-wing) owners, driven as they are by profit and power rather than any sense of building global communications networks which might foster a sense of community. To build a common world requires face-to-face encounters. It also, however, requires finding ways to connect with those in other locations, making visible the entanglements that cross our existences, and using this visibility to dismantle, sabotage and hack these exploitation networks. In this sense, in our work we have developed Hito Steyerl's concept of the 'poor image' a concept she used to refer to the vast circulation of all kinds of moving images through online platforms; sometimes in ways beyond the legal (i.e. a downloaded file of a copy-righted auteur film). To Steyerl, beyond its low resolution or its makers of low quality, the value of the 'poor image' lies in its multiple possibilities for circulating, translating experiences and thus distributing multiple ways of understanding and representing the world. Nowadays it may be difficult to discern what a poor image is, since even relatively low range mobile phones are able to shoot in high resolution and even in 4K. In a way, cheap high-resolution images challenge certain stereotypes about who can produce poor or rich images and force us to rethink what we mean by poor (inequalities must be rendered visible, so they become vulnerable to our attacks). Inequalities amongst images and sounds prevail and poorness emerges even in the sophisticated visual languages that one can or cannot afford to learn in a Film School, as well as in the access to certain means of production, or in the power imbalances inscribed in production processes, the blockade of some products, and the marginalisation of certain kinds of practices and authors.

As a small example, when working in Cuba, this has involved working with Internet connections precarious and expensive for local salaries, which struggle to send and receive small video files. Also, the very practical implications of the us blockade on the island prevents the use of some software commonly used in the West. This technological blockage, though, forces us to find alternatives and learn from the many strategies used by the local population (and the expertise they have developed) to circumvent restrictions.

The Cuban activists in our project coined the term 'Glahamavila' as a utopian festival space connecting all four cities, virtually if not yet physically. Inspired by this small example of reaching towards new futures, we conclude with a third and final reflection on *The Red Paper on Scotland*, one which we had not flagged in the introduction. Despite its limitations, there are many voices within its pages which speak boldly of radical transformation. Since its publication, capitalism has grown increasingly ideologically secure yet increasingly existentially fragile: it seems inconceivable that a strategy for dealing with the 'crisis of all crises', that is climate change, can emerge from within the logics of a system which is oblivious to all but profit margins. As capitalism hurls itself and all the planet on its maniacal death drive, the need to both imagine and build post-capitalist worlds has become increasingly vital, despite all the seeming impossibilities that this entails. For us, though, it is vital to start not with what is possible but with what is necessary.

The Resonance of Music: A Catalyst for Change

Tommy Breslin & Denise Christie

AT ITS CORE, music serves as a powerful mirror reflecting the histories and struggles of working-class communities. It tells our stories and amplifies our demands for political and societal change. Through song, we find an engaging platform to inspire young people to discuss, support, and actively participate in progressive socio-cultural movements. The bond between art and politics is not a modern phenomenon; it stretches back through generations, intertwining creativity with the quest for justice, and Scotland over generations has been no stranger to those bonds.

The arts have always been a vital vehicle for communication, inspiration, and connection among individuals sharing common experiences. They spark debate, challenge the status quo, and bring crucial ideas into the public consciousness. Art encourages society to question preconceived notions and fosters the momentum needed for social change.

In recent years, graffiti has undergone a remarkable transformation in public perception, largely thanks to the enigmatic artist Banksy. His satirical imagery transcends the pages of newspapers and magazines, finding its way onto walls, museums, and auction houses worldwide. Banksy cites inspiration from '3d', a graffiti artist and founding member of the politically charged band Massive Attack. This connection underscores a long-standing relationship between art, popular culture, and protest – a relationship that remains vital today.

Artistic expressions such as Picasso's haunting *Guernica* or Banksy's provocative street art resonate in Scotland. The Scottish graffiti artist Rogue One (real name Bobby McNamara) from Glasgow, has significantly impacted on the street art scene with his vibrant murals and innovative approach, contributing to the city's cultural landscape images that reflect local culture and social themes.

These artists are leaving their mark, just as the music and imagery of Two Tone left its mark on cultural history. The black-and-white checkerboard pattern of Two Tone visually encapsulated the sound behind the records and represented the diverse ethnic make-up of its bands. The Special AKA's anthem 'Free Nelson Mandela' not only propelled an anti-racist message but also showcased how music can serve as a rallying cry for social justice.

Jerry Dammers, founding member of The Specials, remarked that if artists shy away from addressing serious issues, they risk becoming irrelevant, asserting:

> Pop music at its best has always had at least a bit of a connection to the social revolution.

Songs that once inspired generations continue to resonate with today's youth, bridging gaps across time. Consider Billie Holiday's rendition of Abel Meeropol's 'Strange Fruit', whose chilling lyrics demand an end to racism in America. The record cover itself serves as a haunting visual representation of its message – an example of how music can articulate the pain and urgency of social issues.

Music has long been a powerful tool for articulating the challenges, hopes, and aspirations of working people. It unites individuals around shared identities and fosters collective determination to make our voices heard by those in power. From Rock Against Racism in the 1970s to Love Music Hate Racism in more recent years, music has consistently played a pivotal role in combating bigotry and discrimination.

Critics may claim that political songs belong to a bygone era, but this overlooks the vibrant landscape of contemporary music activism. In 2024, artists are once again capturing public attention with their political statements. Take Kneecap – a dynamic hip-hop group from west Belfast that shatters stereotypes surrounding Irish music through their innovative use of cinema. Their work resonates deeply with young audiences in Northern Ireland and beyond.

Similarly, Young Fathers from Edinburgh use their platform to celebrate cultural diversity while challenging both overt and systemic forms of discrimination. Despite their reluctance to be labelled as a political band, their multiracial identity and refusal to conform to norms make them political. Their music subtly addresses social issues, such as Europe's refugee crisis in 'Cocoa Sugar'.

Chvrches lead singer Lauren Mayberry's advocacy against misogyny in music underscores the importance of amplifying women's voices. She uses her platform to address issues such as sexism and abuse within the music industry and founded the feminist collective TYCI in Glasgow which for many years served as a platform for promoting gender equality and supporting women's rights through various initiatives such as live events podcasts and an online magazine. TYCI also provided a space for discussion on activism within the music industry.

In our artistic expressions and daily lives, we must consider how language, imagery, and context convey our messages. A prime example is Tracy Chapman's performance at Wembley Stadium during the Artists Against Apartheid concert – armed only with her voice and acoustic guitar, she addressed an audience of millions with profound impact.

Scottish female musicians have emerged as important advocates for gender equality through their music and activism. Annie Lennox founded The Circle charity to empower women, while Tamara Schlesinger (MALKA) established Hen Hoose – a collective aimed at combating sexism in the industry. Glasgow-based band Brat Coven addresses gender-based violence while promoting inclusivity within their music scene.

Working-class female musicians also play an essential role in Scotland's musical landscape. Punk band Bratakus uses its platform to tackle social issues while gaining traction across Europe. Leah Batty's contributions to alt-rock explore personal themes intertwined with societal challenges. Charlotte Brimner (BeCharlotte) co-founded Enough Records to uplift young female musicians from working-class backgrounds.

Despite these strides, female musicians still confront significant barriers such as misogyny, harassment, gender inequality, and underrepresentation at festivals. Initiatives like Hen Hoose are working tirelessly to promote gender diversity in lineups; however, statistics reveal that women comprised only 33 per cent of performers at Scottish folk festivals in 2023 – highlighting an ongoing disparity.

Brooke Combe is a dynamic Scottish singer-songwriter whose soulful sound is a powerful testament to her commitment to authenticity and representation as a young mixed-race woman in the music industry. Her single, 'Dancing at the Edge of the World,' is a bold declaration of artistic independence following her departure from a major label – a move that challenges the industry's tendency to commodify women for profit. Combe's courageous stand for integrity over guaranteed income is a call to action for audiences to support and elevate artists who prioritise genuine expression over commercial exploitation.

Female musicians have profoundly influenced politics, feminism, and anti-racism efforts in Scotland. Artists like Karine Polwart align their work with political movements advocating for social justice and as alluded to earlier, Lauren Mayberry from Chvrches is renowned for her outspoken stance against sexism within the industry while actively engaging in anti-racism initiatives.

As Paul Simpson (The Wild Swans) aptly stated regarding political lyrics:

For some youngsters the lyrics in a song are secondary to the music…
but for me they are crucial.

He recalls how politicised bands like The Clash provided him with an alternative worldview during his youth amid mass unemployment – a sentiment echoed by many today seeking meaning through music.

Words possess immense power; they can inspire or incite dissent – they can be jewels or ammunition. As Simpson reminds us: 'Don't undervalue or waste your words.' In this era marked by social upheaval and change, let us harness the power of music not just as entertainment but as a formidable force for progress.

Take It Back to the Centre?

Julie McNeill

I'M STANDING IN the Marienplatz, the square in the centre of Munich. It's June 2024 and there are Saltires as far as the eye can see. Crates of beer line the periphery and the dress code is clear: kilts, shorts, Scotland tops.

A young lad of 13 plays the bagpipes and a crowd gathers cheering on every wrong note, giant inflatable footballs drift through the air and there's a sense that this is the start of a four-week party.

'Look, *this is a moment you'll never forget*,' I turn and say to my children who are 10 and 14 years old.

As a Scotland fan there's definitely a sense that you've earned these moments: done the hard yards, witnessed the defeats, freezed your butts off and spent far too much money following the men's and women's teams in every major (and minor) tournament for the past four decades.

I remember feeling exactly like this standing in the rain outside the Parc de Princes in 2019 as we marched to the stadium in Paris with the Tartan Army from a nearby park – my son would've been about 9 years old at the time and had spent the afternoon playing football with new friends from eight different countries. Football – that international language – a free pass to solidarity, rivalry and friendship. We were there to watch the Women's World Cup – Scotland v Argentina.

I remember being outside the stadium as the rain was falling gently in the warm Parisian afternoon and seeing my daughter perched on a kilted man's shoulders, my son laughing in that easy way he used to do before hormones took a hold of him. The traffic had stopped to let us by '*O Flower of Scotland…*' reverberated, this was an effortless joy. The solidarity, optimism, that elation without expectation.

Too often these nights end in disaster – Munich and Paris were no different – but I've never seen people happier to be in the room (or stadium, or country).

Cuthbert and McGinn

At six she slurped Soleros
outside the Parc de Princes
juice dripping stickily down fingers
as her brother climbed,
and skipped, and danced.

They both shouted 'Flower of Scotland'
skin-soaked by Parisian rain
and marched with the Tartan Army,
stopping traffic
with their cheers and waves.

Sat upon a stranger's shoulders
she watched Erin smash it home,
her tummy leapt in expectation
with every cross and throw.
Her brother's leading us to London

crossing numbers off the chart
practicing his 'John McGinn'
in the rain down Barshaw Park.
He'll be singing in Mount Florida
his tummy jittering on the train.

He'll be eating pie and bovril
on the way to Wembley.
And they'll be with us on the sofa
wearing Cuthbert and McGinn

draped in hope and expectation
as we batten down and coorie in.
From Parc de Princes to Hampden
you build it, they will come.

One nation, two teams
and a summer full of dreams.

No Scotland No Party

In the Allianz arena
tears flow unexpectedly
as Flower of Scotland reverberates
around this coliseum.

I cannae believe we are here,
I pull my teenage boy in close
and my heart near bursts.

Three minutes into the game
and an hour after the opening show
two girls announce their arrival

'scuse me, cheers pal
Danke, danke shoen
danke-shoen thank-yer-son'

she shouts in my face –
affectionately – as she passes my boy
small kilts, Saltire faces

and two plastic Proseccos
in each hand balanced perfectly.

As they settle in, apply lippy
take a selfie air kissing each other
in a puff of raspberry scented vapes

Germany score their second
Linda is FaceTiming Shaz who
lives in Coatbridge saying

'That place would be nothing
without you hen.
The heart of the whole company
they'd be fucked without you'

'Stand up if you hate England'
rings out. She stands. Sits.
Then stands.

'Oh fuck I'm confused.
If I stand do I like them?'
The two girls clap along to every chant –
German or Scottish – disnae matter
They make Scott McTominay
fit any melody

On FaceTime they shout loudly
about who the hell would take off
John McGinn and stick on Billy Gilmour?

When Scotland score, one is at the bar
the other on the phone
which is catapulted in the air
like an overhead kick

time seems to slow
as it somehow lands perfectly
on the lap of her red kilt.

Gooooooaaaaalllll

The Germans sing in unison
cheer rhythmically, chant like monks
score five goals, are impenetrable

but as we all know
there's no Scotland no party

Maybe this mass migration to Germany, this madness that swept the country was the distraction we all needed. Is it possible it had little to do with the football?

George Orwell famously talked about football being part of 'a sort of bread and circuses' business 'to hold the unemployed down.' And called it 'an astute move by the governing class', saying

Of course the post-war development of cheap luxuries has been a very fortunate thing for our rulers. It is quite likely that fish-and-chips, art, silk stockings... the movies, and the Football Pools have between them averted revolution.

Is football our circus? Our religion? Our distraction? It's not such a radical idea, many a politician has timed an election announcement or snuck out a bad news story during a major international campaign. Many have tried to ride the optimism, or even take credit for it? Some even pulling on too-tight football tops and awkwardly posing pulling pints 'with the lads'.

Football's roots are of course embedded in our working-class communities, and clubs have had a pivotal role in picking up where politics or community have failed: feeding the hungry; collecting for food and clothing banks; providing exercise and nourishment for children during the long school holidays; championing good causes; providing space for the lonely; addressing and supporting both physical and mental health and, through fantastic initiatives like football memories, using football as the vehicle to bring people together and share experiences and stories. Football clubs are our closed community centres, our empty churches. Making political statements, taking a stand, filling the gap, are all familiar features of our clubs in Scotland.

There are examples of political associations with football throughout our history: *The Blackshirt*, newspaper of the British Union of Fascists, noted in July 1934 that, in Dumfries and Galloway the

Scottish Blackshirts are well to the fore in sports... Next winter there will be at least six Blackshirt football teams in the south of Scotland, and negotiations for a Blackshirt football league are ongoing.

Scottish teams associated with religious or political causes are nothing new. Celtic football club, for example, being founded by Brother Walfrid to feed the hungry of Glasgow's East End:

For Good

On Abercromby Street
The Calton, Glasgow's
East End

brother Walfrid
rejoiced as the young Hibbies
of Edinburgh

brought the Scottish cup home.
He thought whit if our lads
had the same?

A bright new fitba team
wedded from the start
to the common weal:

a hot meal apiece
filling the bellies o the weans
in the East End.

It's the poor look after the poor
in Scotland, always was, and is.
Scottish football is twinned

with good causes from
the Gorbals to Gaza:
The people's game

for the people's good,
let's ne'er forget it.

Clubs founded on principle, with hope, still champion good causes today but there is a polarisation afoot. Just as football can give you a sense of place, of community, of solidarity, so too it can 'other'. I remember someone posing the question to me years ago about Scottish identity saying 'how much of it is tied up with being anything but England?' A confident, secure nation does not need to identify itself by virtue of its neighbours. The late Ludovic Kennedy, in his 1995 book *In Bed with an Elephant* talked about Scotland being suffocated simply by weight of numbers. He said our relationship with the rest of the UK was 'like being in bed with an elephant' – there's nothing wrong with the elephant but it will inevitably crush you.

It was common, for example, in the 1970s to see the Saltire and Union Jack flying alongside each other in support of the national team. Today, in the post-referendum climate, this is a far less common sight. The 'Better

Together' campaign became associated with one flag and Independence with another. Scottish identity as separate from British identity.

This division exacerbates differences at club level, too, where fans fall in behind particular political or global issues by virtue of the fact that their rivals have taken the other side.

Which brings us to the Tartan Army: a fan group which thrives on its reputation as a welcoming, respectful, fun-loving, bagpipe-playing dream of an away support. They spend hundreds of pounds in the local bars, sing in full voice and help grannies across the road. Not to mention the thousands donated through brilliant initiatives like the TA Sunshine Appeal who donate to good causes in every country Scotland plays. The Tartan Army has cultivated this reputation as a force for good, in direct opposition to the media portrayal of England fans abroad.

Scottish football is not without its significant challenges both on and off the pitch. I was recently asked to write poems in response to a football and hate crime project led by universities across the UK including Glasgow Caledonian here in Scotland. I focused on the treatment of women, disabled fans and sectarianism, and the findings were pretty stark! We have a long way to go to create an inclusive environment where fans feel safe and welcome in our grounds, and in our streets and homes, both before, during and after matches.

What I love about football is the ability to keep starting again. Every time the ball goes in the net you go back to that centre spot.

Kickabout

These games are won
and lost in moments
in scuffs and snatches,
trips and pullbacks.

Plant your feet then
raise your heads
and see what you have achieved,
games lost, games won.

Our expectations grow
because you made it so.
Tonight, my daughter watched
you play– she dreams

of being you, one day.
Her jacket's in the wash again,
it's been masquerading
as a goalpost in the mud.

She's ditched the school skirt
for a football strip.
She doesn't measure
her game in inches,

the mud-splats and missed shots
bring her back to the centre spot
where she will rise and fall
and rise again.

So it remains for us to ask: What kind of Scotland do we want to build? My answer would be – an outward-facing, compassionate, socially responsible nation where children don't go to school hungry and are given opportunities to thrive in an education system built for the modern era.

Some might say the chances of achieving this in the age of what looks like austerity mark two are pretty slim but – we're Scottish – four goals down in the Allianz Arena my young lad turned to me and said – 'if we just nicked one back now mum, we'd still be in with a chance.'

While the clock still ticks, there's time to take the ball back to the centre spot, make better use of the talent on the pitch, work together and believe that anything is possible if you work hard and want it enough.

You can't be a football fan without a smidgen of optimism and an overarching sense of hope. There's a lot to be hopeful for in Scotland. We have a beautiful country filled with talent and compassion. I'm excited to see how we grow in confidence with a clear and positive sense of our place in the world.

When Scotland qualified for the Euros these were the odds we were given of winning the competition:

Odds On

Scanning the statistics
in the latest Twitter poll
France's chances are most favourable
followed by Belgium, Spain –
no surprises there.

Scanning down,
down,
down,
a wee bit mair

there's Scotland 0.1% for the win
Hang on, 0.1%?
For the win?
so
you're telling me
there's a chance!

There's always a chance!

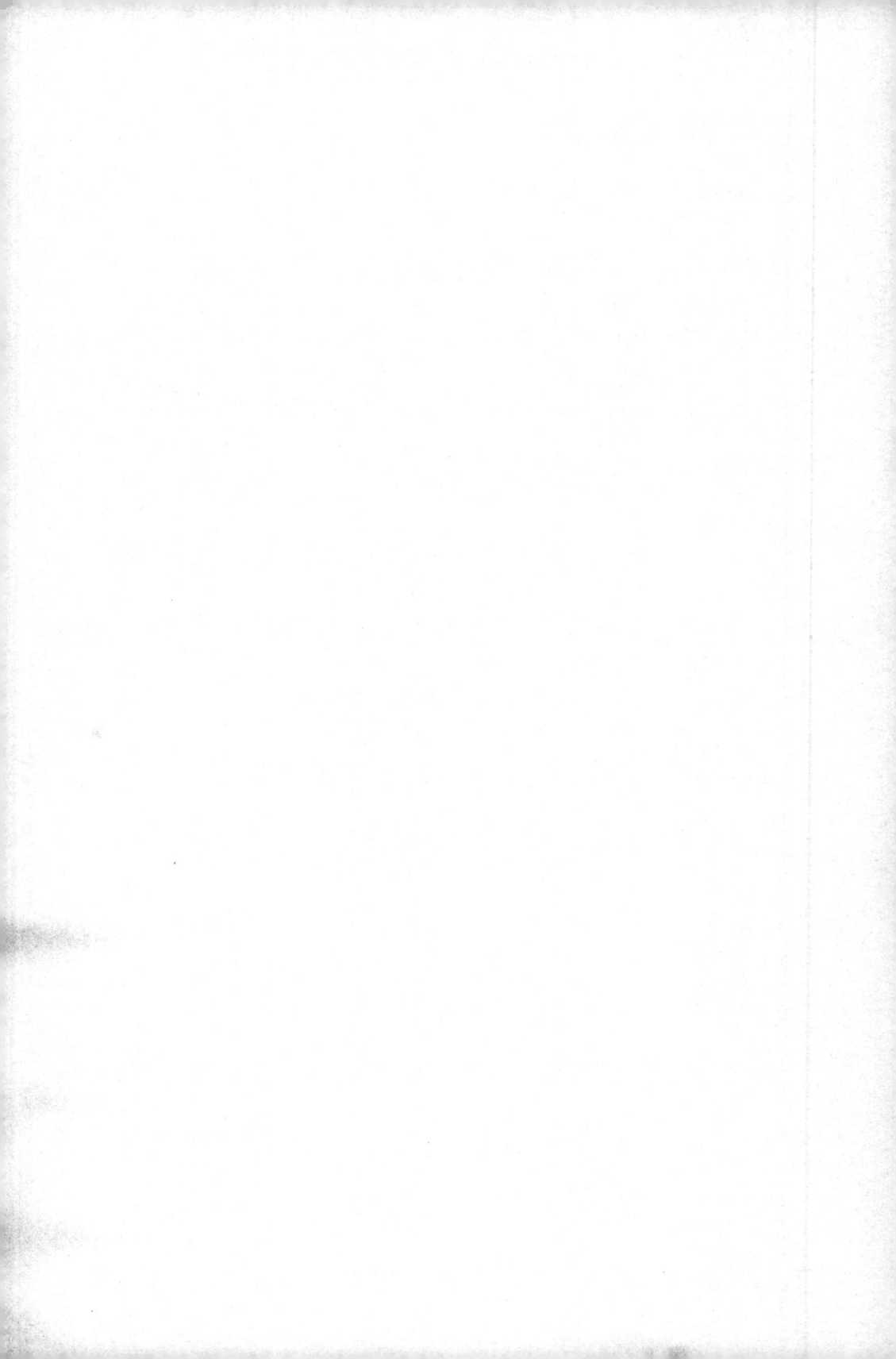

Coda

Our Working-Class Movement –
in What Sense National?

John Foster

THIS CONTRIBUTION CONTINUES a theme first advanced in Gordon Brown's 1975 *Red Paper* and reconsidered in 'Scottish Nationality and the Origins of Capitalism' in Tony Dickson's *Scottish Capitalism* of 1980. Both looked at the origins of the special 'national' features of the Scottish working-class movement and focused particularly on how far Scotland had developed its own capitalist state system and culture before the Union of 1707. Both argued that this process had not been completed and that its fast development thereafter impacted significantly on the subsequent character of class relations.

The argument here does not differ in essence. But it does stress three things.

First, the existence of an earlier commonality of experience between some Scottish regions and Anglo-Saxon England in face of Norman invasion and a level of common resistance to its far harsher militarised and cultural dominance. This was particularly so in the previously Saxon regions of the Lothians, Northumbria and the east coast within what were then politically conjoined Scots and English kingdoms.

However, from the 1200s to the 1540s, it stresses divergence. This is based on more recent research that has highlighted the scale of proto-industrialisation in England. From the 13th century onwards England's export of wool to Flanders was replaced by a state-endorsed policy of domestic cloth manufacturing. The resulting economic transformation – and population growth – was, however, followed a century later by the cataclysmic impact of the Black Death in the mid-14th century.

Scotland saw neither this proto-industrialisation – nor the subsequent population crisis. In England the halving of the labour force brought a doubling of real wages, significant levels of class mobilisation and culturally a reassertion of 'English' language and identity. It also saw a crisis within feudalism in which one faction sought power by alliance with an emergent 'English' merchant class – and an ongoing cultural, religious and organisational dissidence within an increasingly proletarianised labouring population.

Scotland experienced none of this. In the 1200s its Norman rulers seized the opportunity for ending subordination to England, doing so in alliance with Flanders and France, and becoming their replacement supplier of wool. Consequently, Scotland saw no proto-industrialisation, little population increase, a remarkably small incidence of the bubonic plague and none of the proletarian mobilisation seen in England. What conflict did emerge was between an increasingly diversified tenantry and a strongly entrenched Norman Flemish landlord class. This conflict continued unresolved for four centuries – effectively till 1707. This was the great divergence.

It was in consequence of this that the emergent employer class, both in the countryside and towns, faced continually challenged attempts to develop a new state structure that could facilitate capitalist control. It ultimately did so – but in forms that, in turn, gave a number of special characteristics to the emergent working-class movement.

From the mid-16th century these attempts to challenge feudalist demands for centralised, bishop-based control took the form of a highly delegated structure of local presbyteries, councils of local employers/elders, with sweeping powers of control over all aspects of life, of poor relief, reproduction, education and, most important, an imposed ideology that stressed individual conformity to workplace norms.

It was a structure of control that was later vividly lampooned by Robert Burns at a time when it was coming apart. For come apart it did. In the course of relatively rapid industrial development and population growth in the 18th century, congregations rebelled, split, dissented – creating the radical chapels that aligned themselves with the American colonists and later with the still more radical Presbyterians in the north of Ireland.

Hence in thinking about the development of the working-class movement both in Britain and internationally, Scotland's contribution is, for this reason, distinct and important. The first significant attempt at a general strike took place in the west of Scotland in 1820. In 1842 Scottish workers were integral to the first all-Britain general strike. Scotland's Trades Union Councils were formed very early, in the 1840s and '50s, and later played a key role in creating a mass political party for labour in the course of the 1880s and '90s. In 1897 they were instrumental in forming the Scottish Trades Union Congress. Unlike the British TUC, the STUC had specifically socialist objectives from the beginning. In the opening years of the 20th century Scotland was also central to the formation of an all-British shop stewards' movement and, in 1919, 1920 and 1926, to the development of the concept (and reality) of workers' councils and Councils of Action. These councils explicitly sought to unite communities on class terms to challenge capitalist state power. More recently, in the 1960s and '70s, Scottish workers helped lead the way in recreating an all-Britain shop stewards' movement. Over the same period its use of work-ins and occupations and the associated one-day solidarity strikes again broadened the armoury of the British working-class movement and in 1972 saw the demand for 'a workers' parliament' at the first Scottish Assembly.

Yet. Did it, at the time, do so specifically as a 'Scottish' movement? This is the key question posed in this chapter – and the answer given is (mainly) No. There was pride in the achievements of the Scottish trade union and labour movement. But its actions were never, or at least very rarely, conceived in solely Scottish terms. How could they be? State power had by now long been organised at British level. Scottish capital, though often in competition with English and Welsh capital, depended on the joint exercise of that state power against labour.

However, we will also argue that, in one important respect, one determined by the distinct historical development of Scotland's working class, there was a particularly strong emphasis on community-level organisation, on locally uniting the working class as a whole, and that this, while not necessarily unique, did make a specific and sometimes transformative contribution.

Any examination of this general process of working-class development has by its nature to be historical. It took well over three centuries. It drew, as has been noted, on pre-existing national cultures and traditions. And the subsequent lessons drawn had to be worked out collectively. Where effective, these past struggles have been so because the united force of working people broke through the rights of capitalist property, fractured the laws that defended them and did so by mobilising working people across Britain as a whole.

And here, in talking about the working class, we are talking about a class in Marx's terms, defined as all those selling their skills to produce capitalist profit but also, collectively, capable of mobilising this power against capital. And, no less important, being able to do so in the specific national conditions, of Wales, Scotland and England, and drawing on their own *specific* national experiences of class oppression.

This is important today. To a significant extent our country's component national traditions of struggle are themselves now in danger of being turned into something else – into reasons for *rejecting* wider class unity and also, to an increasing degree, for rejecting the millions of working people who have come here from other countries and cultures.

We need therefore to understand these past movements as drawing strength against the power of capital because they represented and united specific national contingents in class terms *as* contingents of *resistance*. And no less important, such cultures of resistance have been strengthened by those who have come here over the last two centuries from Ireland and Eastern Europe and, more recently, from the Indian subcontinent, Africa and the Caribbean.

What follows will be a brief schematic attempt to understand these class linkages – schematic and tentative because the movement that took on Britain's capitalist state was not just operating across the three nations but was also, as Mick McGahey put it, doing so as a 'movement not a monument'. It depended – entirely – on actual people, learning, interacting, passing on their knowledge. And while its settings were national – in terms of Scotland, England and Wales as well as other nationalities – what was learned was often not directly national but about the power of capital in particular industries, about how specific employers operated and about the success and failure of particular responses. Hence, the contacts made were not necessarily seen as 'national' but within individual trade unions, organised across Britain, against encroachments on common rights and in the creation of new vehicles of collective struggle.

We listed some of the achievements of Scottish working people earlier. All were in reality, to a large extent, part of all-British mobilisations in which mutual lessons were learned on tactics and strategy.

So today, in the face of potential and actual class fragmentation, the first step is to win a recognition of this joint struggle against the state power of capital at British level: how it created a working class that gained its collective strength, in part at least, from drawing on these national traditions.

The first section will examine, as already outlined, the distinctive, but to some degree converging, ways in which pre-capitalist, largely feudal state power emerged in both Scotland and England and the perhaps surprising level of *common* resistance to it. The second will look at the 'great divergence' of the five centuries between 1200 and 1700 when England developed dominant capitalist relations of production and Scotland did not. The third will consider the consequences during the fast convergence that followed during the 18th and subsequent centuries and consider how far the legacy of the 'primitive', embattled character of pre-1700 Scottish capitalism, as subsequently carried forward, resulted in turn in a more 'social', community-based understanding of working-class resistance.

'National' identities, 'class' identities and the exercise of state power

> *Since for to defend city*
> *Servants and thralls he made free…*
> *And since off the temple walls tane*
> *The arms their elders bore*
> *And when they armed were and dycht*
> *That stalwart Karls were and wycht*
> *And saw they were free alsua…*
> Barbour's *Bruce*, 1375

> *When Adan delved and Eva span who was then the gentleman?*
> Attributed to John Ball, 1381

These two statements, one Scottish, one English, are separated by less than a dozen years. Notably both were written in a form of English. The quote from John Ball comes from the time of the Peasants Revolt and directly questions the existing social order. The Scottish comes from the court poet of Robert II as Scotland's wars of independence continued. This talks about *past* struggle – how Scots peasants fought to defend their relative freedoms against Viking thraldom three centuries before. Both statements stemmed from, and perhaps reinforced, the cultural identity of those without property in their respective countries. They are therefore relevant to, though they do not explain, the contrasting processes by which feudal class power was overthrown, a new type of capitalist class society emerged and by which a working class was formed.

We will attempt to describe these very different processes – although, in terms of space, our approach has to be drastically schematic.

So, to start with the formation of the 'nations' themselves.

In England this process was relatively straightforward and unitary. By the end of the 600s Germanic invaders had occupied almost all the present-day territory. Some of the pre-existing Celtic peasantry may have been absorbed. But most left – driven to Wales and western coastal areas. A new wave of invaders, the Vikings, arrived in the 800s. However, they did so mainly as slave traders rather than settlers and were met by a relatively coherent response from the English sub-kingdoms, a response that played a major part in creating a more unitary 'national' kingdom. Two and a half centuries later a new invasion took place, the Norman conquest. This again was of a different kind. The Normans sought to institute a new type of feudalism dependent on much tighter, semi-militarised controls – at least in part to maximise income from commercial wool production. Formal serfdom was imposed on a majority of the population. Every effort was made to drive underground existing 'English' identities and language. As we will see, two to three centuries later, the re-emergence of these identities played a significant role in the way in which feudal rule was broken in England and in doing so redefined English identities in new class terms. We will come back to this.

Scotland's development as a nation was more complex. In 600 there were four distinct language groupings. There were largely Christianised Welsh-speaking Britons across most of western flank of Lowland Scotland, Germanic English-speaking settlers in Northumbria, the Lothians and up the east coast, Picts speaking a probably pre-Celtic language occupied most of the landmass north of the Forth and a small enclave of Gaelic-speaking Irish had settled in the far west around Dunadd. All had specific political structures – some tribal or clan, others better described as early-stage feudalism with a settled peasantry, Christian institutions and nobles who drew material tribute or rent.

As in England, the Viking invaders brought unity in resistance – although the process was less coherent. The Vikings sought 'thralls' (slaves) for their lucrative Mediterranean trade. The most immediate challenge was faced by the Irish chieftains of Dal Riada in the West – who were forced to flee east and re-establish themselves across much of the area north of the Forth as 'Kings of the Picts'. During the following two centuries they formed alliances with the English-speaking Northumbrians and the 'Welsh' Strathclyde kings to provide a more coherent resistance and it is to this that Barbour's *Bruce* refers – and, more specifically, does so in terms of defending the relative freedom of settled communities of Christianised peasants, whatever their origins and obligations, from subjection to slavery. Memories of this resistance, therefore, still resonated in the 14th century – even if those who then made use of this rhetoric were themselves French or Flemish feudal nobles who, as in England, represented a harsher, militarised and more exploitative version of feudal rule.

Why did this militarised class of feudal lords decide to cross the Channel from northern France – at the same time as they were battling to occupy central and southern Italy? At least in part the motive seems to have been economic. It was to secure, and expand, the supply of wool from England then woven in the Norman-occupied areas of Northern France and Flanders and marketed through Italy across the Mediterranean. England, and to a lesser extent Scotland, were Europe's main sources of high-quality wool – which, in trading terms, was the medieval equivalent of oil.

Norman military occupation was protracted and bloody. It involved legally and culturally subordinating the existing population, imposing serfdom on a majority (previously little more than a tenth were serfs or slaves) and building the required military and economic infrastructure – castles, fortified trading posts – as well as clearing large tracts of land for sheep.

The process began with the suppression of the 1067–68 Rising of the North. The rising had been led by the surviving English earls and was initially backed by the Scottish King Malcolm II (himself brought up in the English court of Edward the Confessor). Its defeat saw the Normans driving the population from large parts of Durham and northern Yorkshire to create a *cordon sanitaire* with Scotland. A significant number of the English fled north across the then border to Northumbria and the Lothians, English-speaking sub-regions within the Scottish kingdom.

For the pre-existing English population the Norman occupation represented the shattering of a relatively sophisticated and developed society – feudal yes, but one whose evolution still incorporated at least symbolic remnants of the semi-collective institutions inherited from the Germanic tribes and which sustained a (relatively) more calibrated distribution of wealth and power. English now became effectively a proscribed language – one that could paradoxically only be used freely (and legally) in Scotland. The Scottish kings themselves soon became vassals of the Normans and accepted a growing stream of French and Fleming feudal nobles, often from families already based in England, who brought with them Norman expectations of social obedience as well as the monastic institutions needed for the large-scale production of wool.

When we compare the two countries at this stage, during the two centuries of Scotland's vassalage, we find significant similarities as well as some important differences. Scotland remained disproportionately poorer than England. The overall population was probably about 10 per cent of that south of the border but of this the Highlands represented a much larger part of the total and its subsistence economy generated little trade apart from 'black cattle'. Across the Lowlands agriculture was more developed but both soil and climate were considerably less favourable than England's. Sheep, however, were important and represented a major source of commercial income.

Summing up developments up to the end of the 1200s both countries had become subject to a much heavier level of feudal oppression. In England's case this oppression was also cultural and 'national' in terms of the suppression of the English language and culture. In Scotland there remained more diverse nationalities. The new Norman French aristocracy occupied (principally) the Welsh- and English-speaking lands in the Lowlands and Borders. South of the border some element of direct resistance seems to have continued for at least the first generation. The campaign to establish the civil rights of the Anglo-French nobility, the Magna Carta struggles of 1215–25, also saw the resurgence of more plebian movements of 'English' resistance, whose presence is attested by the subsequent 1217 Carta de Foresta, restoring lost economic rights, along with the first of the anti-Norman Robin Hood ballads – ballads also retailed at the time in the English-speaking areas of Scotland. Magna Carta itself also reflected the concerns of the wider 'free' population of merchants and smaller landowners – and, as such, also had legal salience within the vassal state of Scotland. To this extent, political development in these years can be seen as showing that a continuing element of popular opposition to Norman occupation was common to both countries.

The following years, however, from the 1280s onwards, saw economic and political development diverging dramatically – with consequences that continued into relatively recent history and in doing so profoundly marked the emergence of the working class in both countries.

The Great Divergence: the wars of independence and Scotland's wool

The origins of the 'great divergence' are found in a combination of factors:

- a loss of territorial control by England's Franco-Norman monarchs over the textile-producing regions of Flanders and northern France;
- the consequent banning by English monarchs of wool exports at a time when their territories comprised Europe's main sources of high-quality wool: England, Ireland, Scotland and Wales;
- the associated state-sponsored development of weaving and textile production in England;
- a consequent wave of proto-industrialisation which in part resulted in half a century of fast population growth, both urban and rural, but one followed by a staggering reversal from the 1340s when up to half the English population died from the Black Death;
- a resulting drastic change in the balance of power between workers and employers which saw a near doubling of real wages in England over the following century;
- a continuing and deepening crisis within the English feudal system in which new and challenging alliances were formed between commercialising landowners and urban merchants, and what had

been the English underclass, now small-holders and employers of rural labour – alliances that had developed strong 'national' (English) cultural overtones by the later 1300s.

In Scotland none of this happened. Initially, Balliol, the English-backed claimant in the Scottish succession crisis, had enforced Edward I's wool boycott between 1292 and 1296. But by 1306 Robert Bruce had overthrown Balliol, in part using funds and troops supplied by the Flemings and their French allies, and once more opened the export of Scottish wool. The resulting wars of independence lasted for much of the following century and the loss of control by the Norman-Angevin kings to the south.

At least partly as a result there was no transfer to cloth weaving and no proto-industrialisation. Quite the contrary. Scotland remained Flanders' main supplier of wool until the mid-16th century. Scotland's very small population did not significantly grow in the 13th century – but neither did it fall much in the 14th: climatic conditions and a lack of urbanisation meant limited exposure to the Black Death.

However, the wars of independence would never have been won if they had simply been funded through the French/Flemish aristocracy and their cousins in Scotland. Critically, there was a populist anti-feudal element and the wars were fought in ways that had at least something in common with the movements of peasant resistance elsewhere in Europe. In Scotland their success largely depended on the use of guerrilla tactics, the burning of castles, the organising of peasant levies who fought against their own landlords – and subsequently, reflecting this plebian base, the institution of 'archer service' in place of the 'knight-service'. The French nobles sent to Scotland to support the Stewarts later in the 14th century found themselves affronted by the insolent behaviour of the Scottish peasantry.

To that extent the wars represented, as did the popular uprisings in England in the late 1300s, at least a partial repudiation of the Norman 'yoke'. Yet, as noted, the French alliance also had a crippling impact on Scottish economic development. The wool harvest was to be exported entirely – blocking any development of a native textile industry. As a result Scottish towns remained relatively minute and there was no proto-industrialisation of the kind seen in England. Trading activity was concentrated in the ports on the east coast. The wool harvest itself was increasingly bought up in advance in bulk – with universities established in part for the teaching of the Roman law required by external merchants to secure legally enforceable contracts. No less damaging was the long-term tying of Scotland's east coast ports to those of Flanders – a region in decline through most of the 16th century

– rather than to the Atlantic trade that was, by then, providing Portugal, the Netherlands and soon England with the opportunity to profit from a new capitalist type of world commodity market as well as the fruits of external primitive accumulation.

In England the ground for such a transition had been well prepared. The 15th century saw further industrial development, the attraction of artisans from the Low Countries with skills in dying and advanced loom-making, a drastic enfeebling of the old feudal order and a dynastic conflict in which the victorious side was aligned with those forces which wanted to intensify commercialisation. By the 1520s and '30s steps had been taken to seize Church estates and enclose lands – a process of internal 'primitive accumulation' that also aided the century long drive to restore control over labour. By then wages had been brought down closer to their pre-1348 level.

However, the legacy of a century and half of plebian mobilisation remained. Laws passed immediately after the Black Death make it clear that the massive increase in wages was not spontaneous. The most revealing of these Acts was the Fourth Ordinance of 1360 which forbade 'congregations, chapters, ordinances and others' – that is collective organisation. This continued. The 'peasants' revolt' of 1381 was itself the outcome of complex political alliances of rural and urban workers, of small rural employers and town merchants. It was explicitly anti-feudal. It was also assertively 'English' in its challenge to Norman French and closely linked to Lollard demands for an English bible. The first great popular work in English, the *Vision of Piers Plowman*, appeared in the 1380s, a covert denunciation of feudal institutions and a hymn of praise to the 'common' people (the words 'commune' and 'cummuners' are used repeatedly throughout). Through the 15th and 16th centuries there also remained continuing contact with the populist peasant risings and 'utopian' Anabaptist doctrines developing in Germany and central Europe – among a population that was in England becoming both unprecedentedly urbanised and in the countryside increasingly proletarianised. As Christopher Hill stressed in his Collected Essays in a chapter entitled 'From the Lollards to the Levellers', the radical ideologies of the Levellers themselves had a history.

The Levellers in England – and Galloway

Sir, I see that it is impossible to have liberty but all property must be taken away. If it be laid down for a rule, and if you will say it, it must be so. But I would fain know what the soldier hath fought for all this while? He hath fought to enslave himself, to give power to men of riches, men of estates, to make him a perpetual slave.
Reply of the Leveller Leader, Colonel Rainsborough,
to General Ireton: Putney, 29 October 1647

What have we to do in Ireland, to fight and murder a people and nation (for indeed they [the Grandees] are set upon cruelty and murdering poor people which is all they glory in) which have done us no harm...?
The Soldiers Demand, May 1649, when refusing to embark for Ireland

Nothing like the Leveller revolt of the 1640s occurred in Scotland. There was no social basis for it at the time. Although the French grip on state power had been ended in 1560 – both aristocrats and Presbyterians saw advantages to be gained by having a Stuart king in England – Scotland remained held in a gridlock of aborted development. The feudal aristocracy continued to control much of the land – having grabbed at least a portion of that previously in possession of the Church. Urban development remained retarded. Across the Lowlands richer peasants or 'Bonnet lairds', employing a limited number of labourers, had collectively accumulated significant holdings, largely from Church lands. In the still small towns, their equivalents employed handfuls of employees in traditional trades. The Highlands remained self-sufficient, still sustaining a significant population but one largely outside a market economy.

Hence, even after the Union of Crowns in 1603, Scotland's economy remained too underdeveloped to secure significant benefit. Apart from the 1606 grant of a colony in Ireland, the country remained excluded from trade with England's colonies – as well as having itself little to trade apart from wool, coal, salt and cattle. Attempts to interfere in England's internal conflicts in the 1640s and '50s brought further grief. Occupation by Cromwell was followed by partisan intervention from the restored Stuarts which favoured the most reactionary sections of aristocratic power.

Still at this stage the process of proletarianisation had scarcely begun. The feudals wanted labour to mine coal and refine salt for the London markets. Their solution, given Scottish parliamentary approval in 1606, was legal serfdom – tying a refractory population to specific feudal estates. The small employers in the towns and countryside pursued a different approach: the disciplines, and terrors, of Calvinist doctrine – administered by themselves as elders of the Kirk. For over a century aristocrats and Calvinist small employers fought over whether the Church should be ruled by bishops or presbyteries. Specific apprenticed trades did exist. But a 'general' labour force, denied any other source of subsistence, was only in the process of creation.

Yet change was happening. One was *within* Presbyterianism. Though its doctrines and structure were largely designed to 'control' working people, those who made up the congregations were indeed working people themselves and were not necessarily as controllable in the circumstances of relatively fast proletarianisation after 1707. In 1724 the inhabitants of some parishes in Galloway gained notoriety as 'Levellers' by destroying the fences set up by enclosing landlords. A few years later the area Presbytery expelled one of the local ministers for justifying levelling and calling for property to be held in common. Most of his congregation left with him and set up a new Church, nicknamed, after him, the Sandemanians. Congregations then spread across most of the weaving areas of Scotland – Paisley, Dundee, Perth and Glasgow – and subsequently down into England to Newcastle.

Here our story deviates a little – but it does so with a purpose: to illustrate the close interweaving of relations between radical traditions in Scotland and England. One of the Scots who joined the congregation in Newcastle was the father of the proto-socialist Thomas Spence. Spence senior had originally been a netmaker in Aberdeen docks. Here trade union organisation of some sort seems to have existed from the early 18th century at a time when the east coast ports appear to have acted as a transmission belt for trade union ideas and organisation – running down the coast to Dundee, Bo'ness, Leith, Newcastle and on to London, the central destination. Dozens of ships would make the weekly journey. Bo'ness was one of the main Scottish ports for salt and coal and, annually in the 18th century, workers from Bo'ness and the Firth of Forth migrated down to Newcastle for local employment. Here the keel-men, who ferried the coal out to the coaling ships, maintained a high level of union organisation throughout the 18th century.

Spence Senior, we know, held radical opinions. His son published his *Plan* in Newcastle in 1775. This called for a new society in which all land, and all the wealth beneath it, would be held by the people of the parish for common benefit. Spence migrated to London in the 1780s where he became one of the central figures in the London Corresponding Society and in subsequent radical organisations. After his death in 1814 his ideas were carried forward by the Society of Spencean Philanthropists who in 1820 became, mainly by default following the arrests of more leading figures, the residuary organising core for a radical rising in the aftermath of Peterloo. The Spenceans drew on perspectives of mass working-class strike action already rehearsed in 1818 by William Benbow in London and Manchester. In the aftermath of Peterloo their network extended from London to the manufacturing areas of the north and on to the weaving areas of Scotland. Plans for a mass general strike and rising for April 1820 were eventually postponed when it became clear that security had been breached. However, notice of postponement failed to reach some centres in the West Riding and also Scotland. Mobilisation therefore took place in Sheffield and Barnsley as well as, on a larger scale, in the west of Scotland. The Scottish version of the Proclamation for a Provisional Government (there were two others) looks back in history, among other episodes, to the Norman yoke and the winning of the Magna Carta – bringing together, it would seem, memories of common struggle that did indeed, as we have seen, enjoy historical legitimacy and represented a common class heritage.

This story is probably exceptional. But it is one that does nonetheless illustrate potential links between movements in Scotland and England. It also demonstrates the tensions within Presbyterianism. Through the 18th century, as parts of Scotland underwent relatively rapid proletarianisation, secession churches became common and often politically radical. This trend was progressively strengthened through the century under the impact of radical Presbyterianism in America and then in Ireland. Almost all Irish Presbyterians were originally settlers from Scotland and, like Irish Catholics, they were denied civil rights. By the 1780s and '90s, encouraged by the successes of their co-religionists in America, many became engaged in insurrectionary organisation jointly with Catholics. Their ultimate defeat in the 1798 rising saw a significant number seeking refuge in Scotland – some at least later playing an important role in the nascent trade union movement.

This excursion into what may seem like religious history is important. Scotland saw no Levellers in the 17th century. But the materials for their future emergence were present. For it was among the semi-landless, semi-proletarianised general population that the memories of anti-feudal, anti-Norman resistance lived on – sustained by the continued existence of their descendants still ruling vast estates. No less important was the character of the religious settlement in Scotland: a unique form of Presbyterianism that by 1707 had been inscribed in the Union settlement. As we have argued, Scotland's Presbyterian system matched the needs of an embattled employer class in both countryside and the towns, initially small-scale and local, in creating a tractable labour force, a key requirement for further capitalist development. Yet success itself, the creation of a viable proletariat and increasingly large-scale industry, ruptured it in the course of the 18th century. In the key industrial centres secession churches multiplied.

Paisley, as we have noted, was one such area of pioneer industrialisation, developing first linen, then silk and finally cotton spinning and weaving. It witnessed a spate of secession congregations, one of them Glassite, escaping employer control and creating alternative 'social' environments. It also saw what was probably the first large-scale strike among Scottish textile workers in 1773. Their trial heard evidence of 'riotous proceedings which terrified the manufacturers for several weeks'... 'some thousands of useful weavers were engaged in this combination and threatened to go off America in a body'. Somewhat later to maintain their combination the weavers attempted to develop a cooperative manufactory. We see therefore a level of informed resistance – one educated and given confidence, it would seem, by their 'own' social institutions.

This narrative has sought to show the interlinkages between national cultures and, in particular in the case of Britain, illustrate the 'porous' ever-changing character of national identities as a product of social struggle and change. In this case also, as we will note in closing, there was probably a more lasting legacy.

A conclusion?

In seeking a conclusion it is important to identify both what was special and what was common in the 'national' heritages of Scottish and English workers.

We will start by summarising what might be described as specific 'national' features. First, proletarianisation. It began in Scotland much later than in England. It involved different traditions and language groups: Lowland, Irish and Scots Gaels. The process itself was far more brutal immediately, including the destruction of the old Highland economy, amid civil war and forced removal, as industrial development took place. And because subsequent industrial development was itself, in terms of mechanisation and entry to world markets, also later – not by much but enough to matter – Scottish employers in textiles, iron, engineering, and shipbuilding saw themselves at a disadvantage that required lower wages and, if possible, longer hours to compete.

This was important. The framework of contractual relations, which came within Scottish Law, tended to be harsher in its interpretation, and particularly so after the trial of the cotton spinners in 1837. Correspondingly, after the general strike of 1842, it is difficult to identify the same politics of rapprochement and political capture that was very successfully attempted by both government and employers in England. Government commissioners from London may, as in the instance of the mining commission, have advocated this. But there was little response. On the contrary, in the Lanarkshire heartland of heavy industry, coal, iron and later steel, the second half of the 19th century saw a consistent and successful drive to eliminate trade unions. Workers were recruited from Ireland, both Catholic and Protestant, and also the Highlands. Religious differences were exploited. On the Clyde employers were no less aggressive but less successful – largely a result of competition between employers in the face of the cyclical demand for ships and resulting pressures on labour supply. From as early as the 1860s and '70s trade unionists on the Clyde were seeking to unionise all workers, semi and unskilled – a move of significant importance. Still in the following century, in the 1920s and '30s, Scottish employers continued to deploy tactics of artificially created mass unemployment. Maintaining the wage differential continued to be seen as critical by Scottish capital into the second of half of the 20th century.

In terms of the labour response there may also have been special features. Trades Union Councils, providing unity across communities and trades, were established early – in the 1840s and '50s – and intervened powerfully. The role of the *Sentinel*, published weekly by Glasgow Trades Union Council from 1850 to 1865, was remarkable. It was equally remarkable that at least some of the early affiliates of Glasgow Trades Union Council were general or labourers' unions. These perspectives, of local trade union unity, may or may not have derived from the common collectivity in the face of the threats posed by employer aggression, by the absence of a politically co-opted labour aristocracy or as a result of the traditions of radical Presbyterianism – but they continued to be of importance in the formation of the Scottish Labour Party and the STUC. We might also view in the same light the Workers Committee that emerged on the Clyde after 1914 and also the subsequent development, particularly by Gallacher, of the idea of workers' councils post-1918 uniting entire working-class communities, women and men, employed and unemployed, ideas carried forward by his fellow Scot, Robin Page Arnot, in charge, on behalf of the TUC, of the development of Councils of Action in the near revolutionary crisis of 1920, and then redeveloping them in 1926.

There were, therefore, special features in Scotland that would seem to derive from the country's distinctive history in terms of the unfolding of class allegiances and struggles that in turn contributed to the British movement.

Were there common features? For the development of a common 'labour' culture, yes, overwhelmingly. As with the radical political movements from the 1790s onwards, so trade unionists sought all-British unity to prevent employers exploiting divisions. Early examples would be calico printers and hatters in the 1800s, cotton spinners from Ireland, Lancashire and Scotland meeting on the Isle of Mann from the 1820s and coal miners and engineers beginning attempts at all-British unity in the 1840s and 1850s. The Grand National Consolidated Union of the 1830s had sought such unity and the General Strike of 1842 achieved it. In terms of the quest for united Labour parliamentary representation Scottish trade unionists led the way.

So, to end this summing up, it is useful to quote Lenin. In responding to the rise of bourgeois nationalism before the First World War, he wrote in December 1913:

> the elements of democratic and socialist culture are present, if only in rudimentary form, in every national culture, since in every nation there are toiling and exploited masses whose conditions of life inevitably give rise to the ideology of democracy and socialism. But every nation also possesses a bourgeois culture (and most nations a reactionary and clerical culture as well) in the form, not merely of elements, but of the dominant culture... we take from each national culture only its democratic and socialist elements, we take them only and absolutely in opposition to the bourgeois culture and the bourgeois nationalism of each nation.

This essay has tried to identify, in specific form, those elements of national culture which emerged both from struggles against national oppression as well as joint struggles against feudal and capitalist exploitation. Much was indeed specific and national.

By contrast the fetish of unhistorical, static 'nationalisms' deletes this class understanding. Particularly in Britain the real evolution of national identities was porous, dependent on changing levels of common class experience and the balance of class forces. As Lenin stresses, its progressive development depends on understanding these processes and identifying what is democratic and socialist within it and which thereby derives from a common resistance to exploitation and class oppression.

Note on Contributors

NÚRIA ARAÜNA BARÓ teaches Media and Communications Studies at Universitat Rovira i Virgili. DAVID ARCHIBALD teaches Film Studies at the University of Glasgow. They work under the banner, Ragged Cinema, a socialist-feminist film collective. Ragged Cinema is inspired by both Robert Tressell's classic socialist novel, *The Ragged Trousered Philanthropists*, and the term associated with menstruation.

ANDREA BRADLEY is the General Secretary of the Educational Institute of Scotland, the country's largest education union, representing almost 80 per cent of teachers and lecturers across all sectors of Scottish education, at all career stages. Andrea is a former English Teacher.

TOMMY BRESLIN is Senior Development Officer at Scottish Union Learning, increasing trade union led workforce development. Tommy was previously Education Coordinator with Show Racism the Red Card and is now a member of the campaign's Scottish Advisory Committee.

GAVIN BREWIS is a published PhD researcher, member of the Scottish Poverty and Inequality Research Unit, an Associate Member of the Scottish Centre for Crime and Justice Research, and on the Doctoral Research Committee for the Scottish Graduate School for Arts and Humanities.

DENISE CHRISTIE is a retired Firefighter and the first woman elected as Regional Secretary for the Fire Brigades Union in Scotland. Denise served on the fbu's Executive Council and the STUC General Council.

SARA COWAN is Director of the Scottish Women's Budget Group, which aims to deliver a gender-equal economy. Sara previously worked at Oxfam and started her career as an independent advocate for people with mental and physical health difficulties.

PETER DUFFY is a Scottish Labour activist and campaigner based in Glasgow. Peter is secretary of Campaign for Socialism and a member of the Red Paper Collective.

KATRINA FACCENDA is a Labour councillor representing Leith Ward in Edinburgh, Co-Convenor of the Campaign for Socialism and works in the tourism industry.

JOHN FOSTER published *Class Struggle and the Industrial Revolution* in 1974 on the development of the English working class and subsequently, with Charles Woolfson, studies of the Upper Clyde Shipbuilders Work-in, the Caterpillar Occupation and the Oil Workers strikes of 1991–92.

SUSAN GALLOWAY has worked in research roles in the children's sector, local government, higher education and the trade union movement for over 30 years. Susan is a former Scottish Secretary of the Communist Party of Britain.

ROSIE HAMPTON campaigns for a just transition away from fossil fuels at Friends of the Earth Scotland. Rosie also has a PhD from the University of Glasgow, examining left-wing spaces in 1980s Scotland.

LYNN HENDERSON is Chief of Staff (Operational) at the Public and Commercial Services Union. Lynn is also Chair of the Electoral Reform Society and of the Jimmy Reid Foundation, a Scottish left-wing progressive think tank.

SALVADOR ALLEN HUGHES is a lawyer with a particular interest in constitutional reform and devolution.

DIARMAID KELLIHER is a human geography lecturer and UCU representative at the University of Glasgow. Diarmaid is author of *Making Cultures of Solidarity: London and the 1984–5 Miners' Strike*, Routledge, 2021 and is currently writing a history of picketing.

MATT KERR has been a Labour councillor in Cardonald, Glasgow, since 2007. A past convenor of social care and member of NHS greater Glasgow and Clyde health board, Matt has since 2023 been Scotland reporter for the *Morning Star*.

COSTAS LAPAVITSAS is Professor of Economics at the School of Oriental and African Studies. In January 2015 Costas was elected in the Greek Parliament. His most recent book is *The State of Capitalism*, with the ERENSEP Collective, Verso, 2023.

RICHARD LEONARD has been a member of the Scottish Parliament since 2016, and was leader of the Scottish Labour Party from 2017–20. A former economist at the STUC and trade union organiser, he has written extensively on the Scottish economy for the last 30 years.

STEPHEN LOW is a trade union researcher and Labour Party member. Formerly a journalist with the BBC, Stephen writes regularly for the *Morning Star*.

COLL MCCAIL is a freelance writer based in Glasgow. Coll is a member of Progressive International's Secretariat and edits Skotia.

JULIE MCNEILL is the Poet-in-Residence for St Mirren Football Club Charitable Trust and The Hampden Collection. Julie is the author of *Mission Dyslexia* and poetry collections *Ragged Rainbows*, *Something Small* and *We Are Scottish Football*.

VINCE MILLS is a founder member of the Red Paper Collective and edited *The Red Paper 2005*. Vince is joint secretary of Radical Options for Scotland and Europe and in the Campaign for Socialism. He writes for the *Morning Star*.

JAMES MITCHELL is Professor of Public Policy at Edinburgh University having previously held chairs in Politics and Public Policy at the Universities of Sheffield and Strathclyde. James has written extensively on the relationship between constitutional politics and public policy.

SUSAN MORRISON is a writer, broadcaster and comedian. She doesn't do biographies. She isn't that interesting. But her work is.

TOM MORRISON is Secretary of Clydebank Trade Union Council, Retired member of unison and member of unite Community. Tom is a member of the Communist Party.

FRIEDA PARK is a writer and activist. She is involved in peace and solidarity activity, particularly in relation to Cuba and Venezuela. Frieda writes about global imperialism and the resistance to its domination and drive to war.

DAVE WATSON is the Director of the Jimmy Reid Foundation, former head of policy at unison Scotland and author of several papers on public service reform. Dave was also an expert advisor to the Christie Commission on public service reform.

ARTHUR WEST was Joint Staff Trade Union Convener East Ayrshire Council and is currently Secretary of East Ayrshire Trades Union Council and Secretary of Ayrshire CND. Arthur is active in Don't Bank on the Bomb Scotland and Scottish Trade Union Peace Network.

Some other books published by **LUATH PRESS**

'Mon The Workers
Daniel Gray
ISBN 978-1-80425-033-4 PBK £12.99

Collier Laddie
Rab Wilson
ISBN 997-1-80425-134-8 PBK £9.99

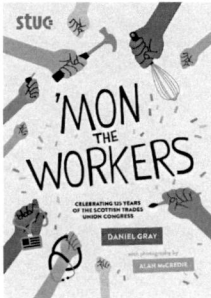

The postman and the primary teacher, the midwife and the musician. Workers in shops, workers at sea. Solidarity with the Columbian farmer and the Palestinian fireman...

Modern trade unionists in Scotland perform roles in every imaginable location and are drawn from all backgrounds. They campaign to win on issues facing the colleague next to them or a comrade thousands of miles away. *'Mon the Workers* tells their stories in their own words. It is a celebration of 125 years of the STUC, and a clarion call for the next generation to agitate, organise and win.

'Mon the Workers should grace the shelves of union offices across the country... well worth reading and well worth returning to as a resource.
STUART FAIRWEATHER, DEMOCRATIC LEFT SCOTLAND

'Mon the Workers is not just a piece of commemorative history. It's also part of the organiser's toolkit. The power of these stories is that they are told by workers in their own voices.
JENNI GUNN, SCOTTISH LEFT REVIEW

Forty years on from the 1984–85 UK Miners' Strike, the largest union-led industrial action in the 20th century, Rab Wilson – a former miner deeply entrenched in the strike – delivers a powerful narrative through his mining poems and strike diary, addressing contemporary social and economic issues in Scotland and the UK then and now.

Having toiled in Scotland's mining industry for eight years, Rab provides an authentic voice that resonates with the struggles faced during the strike, vividly captured from his involvement between 12 March 1984 and 5 March 1985. This book serves as a testament to the working-class struggle, offering a unique perspective on the historical significance of Scotland's mining industry, skilfully expressed by a poet intimately connected to it. Rab Wilson emerges as an essential chronicler, ensuring the legacy of the miners' challenging strike endures in the pages of this evocative and timely work.

Collier Laddie is an ode to resilience, solidarity and the enduring legacy of those who fought for justice during a pivotal moment in industrial history.

What Would Keir Hardie Say?
Exploring Hardie's vision and relevance to 21st century politics
edited by Pauline Bryan
ISBN 978-1-910745-15-1 PBK £9.99

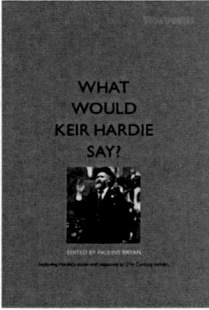

Keir Hardie and the 21st Century Socialist Revival
edited by Pauline Bryan
ISBN 978-191302-503-8 PBK £9.99

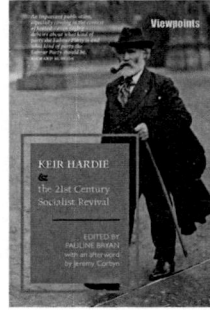

My work has consisted of trying to stir up a divine discontent with wrong.—KEIR HARDIE

Has the Labour Party stayed true to Hardie's socialist ideals and vision?

What would Hardie make of the recent developments in Scottish politics?

If he were active today, what would Keir Hardie say about attacks on welfare; trade union rights; immigration; privatisation; European Union; the economy?

A passionate leader who fought for justice, Keir Hardie, founder and first leader of the Labour Party, was a stringent critic of the world he saw around him. A socialist, a trade unionist and above all an agitator, he gave unstinting support to the women's suffrage movement and risked all in his commitment to anti-imperialism and international peace.

Now, 100 years after Hardie's death, editor Pauline Bryan gathers together essays from writers, trade unionists, academics and politicians to reflect on Hardie's contribution and what it means today.

To remember Hardie is not to look wistfully backwards but to remind ourselves of the absolute necessity of unflinching principles, vision and determination in looking forward to the future we want to build—RICHARD LEONARD

James Keir Hardie founded and was the first leader of the Labour Party. In this book, Pauline Bryan brings together a varied group of commentators to discuss his legacy, including MPs Jeremy Corbyn and Richard Burton; Richard Leonard MSP; Ann Henderson, the Rector of the University of Edinburgh; and Sharon Graham, Executive Officer of Unite. In their fascinating and varied essays, each contributor shows the importance of using Hardie's legacy as a foundation for the future. Discussing his support for women's suffrage and his fight to tackle unemployment, as well as his stance on issues of Home Rule and the British Empire, here they show how intrinsic his beliefs are to Labour Party politics to this day.

Never has socialism been more relevant; only by providing for need not greed can we eliminate poverty and ensure the sustainability of our precious planet. Hardie taught us much, above all, that his staying power against adversity could bring about change.—JEREMY CORBYN MP

Homage to Caledonia
Scotland and the Spanish Civil War
Daniel Gray
ISBN 978-1-913025-36-6 PBK £12.99

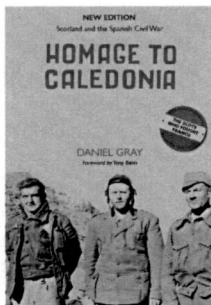

Our Fathers Fought Franco
Scotland and the Spanish Civil War
edited by Willy Maley
Willy Maley, Tam Watters, Lisa Croft, Jennie Renton
ISBN 978-1-80425-040-2 PBK £12.99

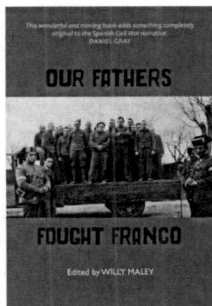

The Spanish Civil War was a call to arms for 2,300 British volunteers, of which over 500 were from Scotland. The first book of its kind, *Homage to Caledonia* examines Scotland's role in the conflict, detailing exactly why Scottish involvement was so profound. The book moves chronologically through events and places, firstly surveying the landscape in contemporary Scotland before describing volunteers' journeys to Spain, and then tracing their every involvement from arrival to homecoming (or not). There is also an account of the non-combative role, from fundraising for Spain and medical aid, to political manoeuvrings within the volatile Scottish left.

Daniel Gray's important and powerful book Homage to Caledonia *tells the story of those deeply committed and courageous Scots who volunteered to fight for democracy and socialism against General Franco and his forces.*
TONY BENN

Told through the words and experiences of those who were there, this meticulously researched and beautifully written book is simultaneously heart-breaking and uplifting.
MAGGIE CRAIG

A resonant piece of working-class history, this book is a living link to four extraordinary stories. Why did these young men put their lives on the line and go to Spain to fight with the International Brigades? How did they all end up in the same prison cell? And what is their legacy today?

There was no good speaking of the menace of fascism, and not going to fight it myself.
JAMES MALEY, GLASGOW

There was the sense of freedom in the air, of workers' power.
DONALD RENTON, PORTOBELLO

You fight for your beliefs, not medals.
GEORDIE WATTERS, PRESTONPANS

There have been reports that [when we were released] we shouted 'Long Live Franco'. Not on your life!
ARCHIBALD CAMPBELL McASKILL WILLIAMS, PORTSMOUTH

Each of the authors calls us to read the signs for our own times in the legacy of these men of the IB.—LESLEY ORR, *Bella Caledonia*

Details of these and other books published by Luath Press can be found at:
www.luath.co.uk

Luath Press Limited

committed to publishing well written books worth reading

LUATH PRESS takes its name from Robert Burns, whose little collie Luath (*Gael.*, swift or nimble) tripped up Jean Armour at a wedding and gave him the chance to speak to the woman who was to be his wife and the abiding love of his life. Burns called one of the 'Twa Dogs' Luath after Cuchullin's hunting dog in Ossian's *Fingal*. Luath Press was established in 1981 in the heart of Burns country, and is now based a few steps up the road from Burns' first lodgings on Edinburgh's Royal Mile. Luath offers you distinctive writing with a hint of unexpected pleasures.

Most bookshops in the UK, the US, Canada, Australia, New Zealand and parts of Europe, either carry our books in stock or can order them for you. To order direct from us, please send a £sterling cheque, postal order, international money order or your credit card details (number, address of cardholder and expiry date) to us at the address below. Please add post and packing as follows: UK – £1.00 per delivery address; overseas surface mail – £2.50 per delivery address; overseas airmail – £3.50 for the first book to each delivery address, plus £1.00 for each additional book by airmail to the same address. If your order is a gift, we will happily enclose your card or message at no extra charge.

Luath Press Limited
543/2 Castlehill
The Royal Mile
Edinburgh EH1 2ND
Scotland
Telephone: 0131 225 4326 (24 hours)
Email: sales@luath.co.uk
Website: www.luath.co.uk